●═ RE-CREATING TEAMS DURING TRANSITIONS

A Practical Guide To Optimizing Team Performance During Changing Times

Paul J. Jerome

Richard Chang Associates, Inc.
Publications Division
Irvine, California

Re-Creating Teams During Transitions

A Practical Guide To Optimizing
Team Performance During Changing Times

Paul J. Jerome

Library of Congress Catalog Card Number
94-69227

© 1994, Richard Chang Associates, Inc.
Printed in the United States of America

ISBN 1-883553-58-X

Richard Chang Associates, Inc.
Publications Division
41 Corporate Park, Suite 230
Irvine, CA 92714
(800) 756-8096 • Fax (714) 756-0853

ACKNOWLEDGMENTS

About The Author

Paul J. Jerome is Vice President of Richard Chang Associates, Inc., a diversified organizational improvement consulting firm based in Irvine, California. He is an experienced management consultant and business executive specializing in executive development, management training, team building, and performance management. Paul is widely recognized for his creative design and enthusiastic delivery of practical management tools and techniques.

The author would like to acknowledge the support of the entire team of professionals at Richard Chang Associates, Inc. for their contribution to the guidebook development process. In addition, special thanks are extended to the many client organizations who have helped us shape the practical ideas and proven methods shared in this guidebook.

Additional Credits

Editor: Sarah Ortlieb Fraser

Reviewer: Cathy Bolger

Graphic Layout: Suzanne Jamieson

Cover Design: John Odam Design Associates

PREFACE

The 1990's have already presented individuals and organizations with some very difficult challenges to face and overcome. So who will have the advantage as we move toward the year 2000 and beyond?

The advantage will belong to those with a commitment to continuous learning. Whether on an individual basis or as an entire organization, one key ingredient to building a continuous learning environment is *The Practical Guidebook Collection* brought to you by the Publications Division of Richard Chang Associates, Inc.

After understanding the future *"learning needs"* expressed by our clients and other potential customers, we are pleased to publish *The Practical Guidebook Collection*. These guidebooks are designed to provide you with proven, *"real-world"* tips, tools, and techniques—on a wide range of subjects—that you can apply in the workplace and/or on a personal level immediately.

Once you've had a chance to benefit from *The Practical Guidebook Collection*, please share your feedback with us. We've included a brief *Evaluation and Feedback Form* at the end of the guidebook that you can fax to us at (714) 756-0853.

With your feedback, we can continuously improve the resources we are providing through the Publications Division of Richard Chang Associates, Inc.

Wishing you successful reading,

Richard Y. Chang
President and CEO
Richard Chang Associates, Inc.

TABLE OF CONTENTS

"Progress is impossible without change, and those who cannot change their minds cannot change anything."

George Bernard Shaw

'There is nothing wrong in change if it is in the right direction. To improve is to change, so to be perfect is to have changed often."

Winston Churchill

"The art of progress is to preserve order amid change and to preserve change amid order."

Alfred North Whitehead

CHAPTER ONE

INTRODUCTION

Creating and maintaining high performing teams is crucial in today's competitive business environment. Indeed, efficient and effective teams can account for the difference between an organization that just barely survives and one that thrives.

Ineffective Team

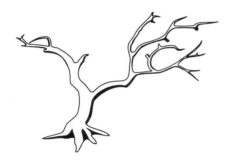

High Performing Team

It is therefore critical that all members of the organization think and make decisions as if they were smart business owners. Each team member must view him or herself as a valuable resource and be proactive in the creation and re-creation of high quality teams in periods of transition.

Why Read This Guidebook?

Change is a constant. And teams need a way of dealing with it. This guidebook features a four-phase model to help guide teams in transitions.

Teams must respond quickly to various challenges that frequently arise when an organization experiences:

Transitions That Challenge Teams

⇗ **growth**

⇗ **downsizing**

⇗ **reorganization**

⇗ **mergers and acquisitions**

⇗ **redirections in strategic and/or operating plans**

⇗ **changes in leadership**

⇗ **shifts in team membership** (*due to a promotion, transfer, new hire, resignation, leave of absence, retirement, termination, etc.*)

This guidebook presents a systematic approach to help ensure that your organization's teams continue to deliver high quality performance before, during, and after an organizational change.

The benefits from following a plan, include:

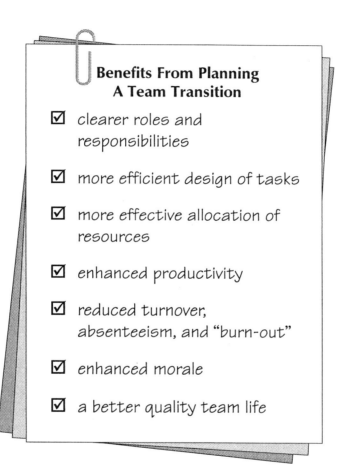

**Benefits From Planning
A Team Transition**

☑ clearer roles and responsibilities

☑ more efficient design of tasks

☑ more effective allocation of resources

☑ enhanced productivity

☑ reduced turnover, absenteeism, and "burn-out"

☑ enhanced morale

☑ a better quality team life

Whether you are a team member, team leader, or a Human Resources professional, you will be able to use the forthcoming checklists and worksheets to successfully plan, implement, and evaluate team transitions.

Who Should Read This Guidebook?

Supervisors, managers, and team leaders and members will gain
valuable tools to successfully guide teams through transitions.
Indeed, maintaining high quality teams is everyone's responsibility
from the front-line employee to the owner.

This guidebook is also valuable to professionals in the fields of
Human Resources, Training and Development, Organizational
Development, and Total Quality Management. With these practical
tools and techniques, you will be able to assist transitioning teams
in attaining and maintaining their fullest potential.

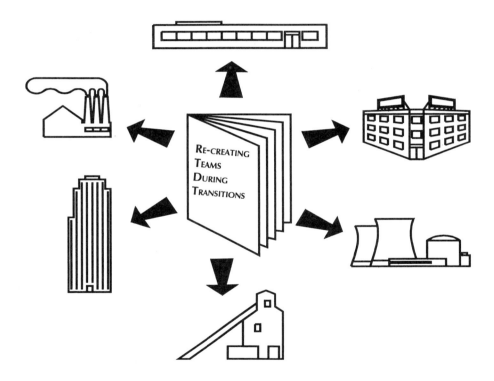

The checklists and worksheets in this guidebook can help anyone
associated with teams, whether it be in small or large organizations,
profit or nonprofit. The tools and concepts presented are useful in
all industries, from banking and manufacturing to education and
government.

When And How To Use It

Use this guidebook whenever you are involved with a team in transition. In today's highly competitive, rapidly changing business environment, team transitions are a nearly continual phenomenon. You'll find the guidebook a valuable resource for teams of few members all the way up to transitions involving hundreds of team members.

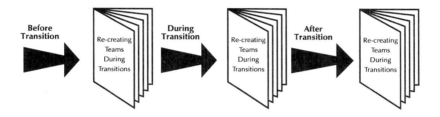

Through the use of the Team Transition Worksheet introduced in this guidebook, everyone associated with team performance can act as a valuable resource, before, during, and after a transition. Use the Reproducible Forms in the Appendix to involve everyone in the process of successful team transitioning.

Also, you will find a summary worksheet at the end of each chapter. These wroksheets will help you apply the concepts in *Re-creating Teams During Transitions* to your situation.

To learn about ways to maximize the potential of your organization, look at the other titles in the Practical Guidebook Collection listed at the end of this guidebook.

Setting The Stage For A Successful Transition

 "The world doesn't fear a new idea.

What it fears is a new experience."

D.H. Lawrence

What To Expect During Changing Times

Ever-changing roles and expectations. Conflicts with new directions and old methods. Endless questions without answers. They will all be there. So will their impact. And so will you.

A team transition often generates a great deal of emotion. These feelings range from excitement and enthusiasm to apprehension, sadness, and anger.

The resulting behaviors also range from welcoming the changes with open arms to confusion, resistance, or apathy. And in some cases, such as during a company layoff, employees may even try to sabotage transition efforts.

Addressing the emotional aspects of change (*e.g., overcoming resistance to change, managing group dynamics, etc.*) and promoting team building (*e.g., sharing performance feedback, developing problem solving skills, etc.*) are critical. These concerns, however, are covered in detail in other guidebooks in the Practical Guidebook Collection.

This guidebook emphasizes the *"what-to-do"* and the *"how-to-do-it"* of managing successful team transitions. It addresses what all team members can do before, during, and after a team transition to help ensure success. Therefore, only an overview of what to expect and how to respond to team transitions will be necessary.

Nearly all organizational changes produce similar challenges and opportunities. They include:

☞ **Rising concerns**

☞ **Overlooked issues**

☞ **More opportunities**

Rising concerns

During any transition, you can expect concerns, questions, and anxieties to arise due to a great number of changes, unknowns, and ambiguities in a short period of time. There will be differences of opinion. There will be conflicting priorities. You should expect some chaos.

Overlooked issues

Your organization, managers, and team members may overlook some issues during a team transition. It will be difficult to anticipate everything that may occur.

More opportunities

More than ever, each team will rely on the skills, ideas, and support of all of its members—its most valuable resources.

How To Respond As A Smart Business Owner

No one will have all the answers. As a team leader or member, you are likely to have the best understanding of what is required for you and your team to be successful. So let's just get right to the bottom line.

When in doubt, be smart and act as though you own the business.

HOW TO BE A SMART BUSINESS OWNER

☑ Get involved *now*

☑ Understand the *"big picture"*

☑ Clarify management's expectations

☑ Establish plans and goals

☑ Manage work efficiently and effectively

☑ Provide solutions

☑ Assist others unselfishly

☑ Remain flexible

Get involved *now*

Act. Don't wait for someone else to act or ask. Your direct and immediate involvement is necessary for continuous improvement efforts to succeed. And your interest can be infectious.

You will minimize problems by involving all team members in the coordination of a team transition. You will also reduce confusion and resistance. Help team members feel informed of what is happening as well as where they are headed.

Understand the *"big picture"*

To make sound business decisions, you have to know where your organization is going and why. Ask. Do some research. Use your influence.

Find out about the health and future of your industry, your organization, and your team. Seek strategic plans—visions, missions, values, goals and objectives that can give you insight into what is needed tomorrow *today*.

Clarify management's expectations

Work together and ask for guidance from management in making decisions in this time of shifting roles and responsibilities.

For example, ask your team leader how he/ she would prefer you and your team to deal with decisions *"on the fly,"* when there's no time for a team meeting. Is it better to ask for permission or forgiveness? When in doubt, act with common sense first and then immediately discuss your actions with your team leader and members.

It is as crucial for management to be supportive as it is for team members to be proactive in asking for management support.

Establish plans and goals

The key to a successful team transition is planning with a vision. Rather than waiting for someone else to come up will the *"overall master plan for heaven and earth,"* immediately get involved to create and implement a team-based transition plan. And instead of changing just to do things differently, have a goal in mind. Know what you're trying to accomplish.

There are many techniques and considerations for planning an organizational transition that will minimize the confusion and frustration that often accompany it. Try some out. You'll find many such ideas in this guidebook. By implementing a systematic approach to team transitions, you can maximize the treatment of all employees as valuable resources and minimize the possibility of things *"falling between the cracks."*

Manage work efficiently and effectively

All transitions can open doors and have trap doors. Take them by the handle—identify challenges and ways to overcome them and identify opportunities and ways to capitalize on them.

Help plan, negotiate, and reassign team duties as requirements and needs continue to change. Allocate time and resources in the most cost-effective manner possible.

Provide solutions

Management will not have all the answers during an organizational change. This is not meant to be disrespectful, just realistic. Their hands will be full as they juggle strategic and

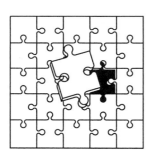

operational priorities. However, you can throw them another ball or lend them another hand.

Expect that questions will far outweigh answers in the short-term. Therefore, it is in your and the organization's best interests to include suggestions, recommendations, and solutions with all of your questions.

Which ideas will get the most attention? Those process improvements that streamline operations and optimize the use of your team's resources.

Assist others unselfishly

Be open and positive when taking on additional responsibilities for periods of time. Be available to assist others at their convenience. Don't worry about *"what's in it for me"* in the short-term.

Most importantly, if you don't promote yourself over others and don't complain, your efforts *will* be noticed and remembered.

Remain flexible

Team members will have different *(often conflicting)* needs and interests. And they won't all be clear at first. Be sensitive and patient as you discuss them.

Since no one can anticipate everything, don't try to come up with the *"perfect plan,"* the *"final draft"*—the concrete for your tombstone! Things will change again. Likely tomorrow. What you need is a process for handling the changes as your team continually strives to achieve its goals. And a willingness to do whatever it takes to get that job done.

Be more tolerant of questions and mistakes. It will take time for everyone to learn new expectations, systems, and skills. If someone makes an error but shows initiative, reward the effort and discuss ways to handle the situation differently in the future.

CHAPTER TWO WORKSHEET: OVERCOMING CHALLENGES AND CAPITALIZING ON OPPORTUNITIES

Use the following questions to help complete the worksheet, *"Setting The Stage For A Successful Transition."*

1. What transition is your team experiencing (*e.g., growth, downsizing, reorganization, merger, acquisition, redirection in strategic and/or operating plans, changes in leadership, shifts in team membership due to a promotion, transfer, new hire, resignation, leave of absence, retirement, or termination, etc.*)?

2. What are the goals of your team's transition (*i.e., what are you, your team, and the organization trying to accomplish*)?

3. What do you anticipate will be the greatest challenges during the upcoming transition?

4. How can you overcome these challenges?

5. What do you anticipate will be the greatest opportunities during the upcoming transition?

6. How can you capitalize on these opportunities?

7. What support do you need from others (*e.g., management, other teams, the team leader, etc.*) to ensure a successful team transition?

8. What will *you* specifically do to *"act as a smart business owner"* and assist your team through the transition?

Feel free to add to this worksheet later following a discussion with your team.

SETTING THE STAGE FOR A SUCCESSFUL TRANSITION

1. Transition	2. Goals
3. Challenges	4. Ways to Overcome
5. Opportunities	6. Ways to Capitalize
7. Support Needed	8. What I Will Do

APPLYING A TEAM TRANSITION MODEL

 "Never underestimate the value of a change strategy. It can help you get through the whole thing a lot quicker than if you just let it happen to you."

-experienced team member in transition

What To Learn From The Past

The successes and disappointments of past team transitions are a valuable learning tool for future transitions.

Planning the wrong thing

Jan is taking a six-month leave . . .

of absence to finish her degree. Along with her many other responsibilities at FurniSure Enterprises, a manufacturer of fine office furniture, she is the only team member skilled in generating the computer reports on available inventory. It would take at least two weeks to train someone to do this task. In addition, Jan will not be replaced in her absence and other team members are already feeling overloaded.

Team members have planned a party for Jan on her last workday. In a meeting the day before the party, one of Jan's coworkers, Tony, asked who will be taking over Jan's responsibilities. The team leader replied, *"Let's all pitch in and take on a part of Jan's responsibilities. Tony, why don't you take on the inventory reports?"* Tony's jaw hit the floor. . . .

What happened? Jan's coworkers were excited about this great opportunity for her. They did a great job planning for a celebration. But now they're in distress. No one thought to plan the transitioning of her responsibilities. Instead, they opted for a typical *"no-brainer"* solution and made the most common error— they *"blindly"* reassigned the responsibilities *"as is"* without discussion.

If only someone had earlier asked, *"What is the best way to handle Jan's responsibilities in her absence? Is it possible to eliminate a task or two while the door is open and we have fewer staff? Can we redesign her duties in any way to make them easier to handle while we have this chance? Or, must some tasks be reassigned 'as is'? Can we change our own roles and reshape a few responsibilities to free up time to assume some of Jan's assignments? How can we most effectively use Jan's skills and knowledge before she goes on leave? Who can she train to cover her job in her absence?"*

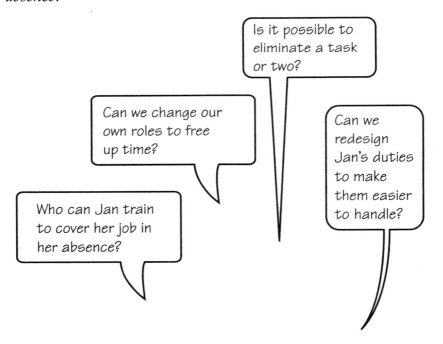

But now it's too late. All they ask is, *"Can I have another piece of cake?"* Nothing's wrong with dessert, unless it's taking the place of a balanced meal or plan.

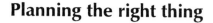
Planning the right thing

Sometimes we can pick up good pointers from those outside our playing field.

An NFL starting quarterback, Joe, will be . . .

having an unexpected operation on his back that will take him out for the remainder of the season. The coach starts looking at options for a successful team transition from the moment he finds out about the operation.

Instead of using the same playbook *'as is' (with fewer resources, i.e. without Joe)*, the coach considers the following: *What plays should we immediately eliminate from our repertoire? How can we adjust our play selection to better fit the different skills and experience of our second-string quarterback? What plays must we rely on 'as is' (e.g., the running game that doesn't rely so much on the quarterback)? What if Joe's recovery is slow? Should we trade for another starter or back-up quarterback with another team? How much time will the team need to adjust to a new quarterback? How can we best utilize Joe before and after his operation (e.g., as a temporary assistant quarterback coach)?*

Preparation for the transition starts right away. The coach leaves as little as possible to chance. He examines all options and uses all resources effectively. All players are actively involved. There are no surprises— except for the party the players throw for Joe at the hospital!

Why was *this* team transition so carefully planned? After all, this change *(Joe's injury)* was unexpected.

Yes, everyone wanted to maintain high quality team performance. But it's deeper than that. The coach and the players were thinking and acting as smart business owners. After all, the coach's and players' jobs *(and their future earning potential)* rely on the team continuing to do well. This is not so different from any other competitive business environment!

Some of the phases the coach and his players went through are worthy of note.

How To Model Success In The Future

This guidebook provides a systematic approach to team transitions that allows for total team involvement. The process will help ensure that you use all resources to their fullest potential during all phases of the transition. You will achieve shared goals—a primary goal of any smart business owner.

We will look at the four phases of successful team transitions.

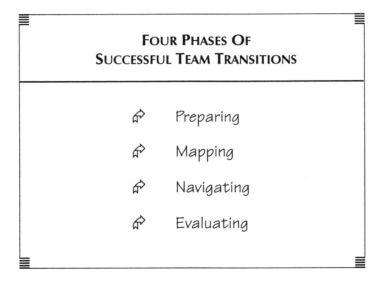

FOUR PHASES OF
SUCCESSFUL TEAM TRANSITIONS

⇪   Preparing

⇪   Mapping

⇪   Navigating

⇪   Evaluating

Planning a successful team transition is much like planning a successful trip or journey. Both begin with early preparation and mapping of the course, followed by navigating and evaluating the trip.

PREPARING

EVALUATING — MAPPING

NAVIGATING

Early preparation involves a bit of goal-setting (*e.g., deciding where to go, how long it will take, and who will go along*). Mapping the course involves detailed planning of the best way to get to your destination. Paying thorough attention to the map helps ensure smooth navigating. As the trip begins, you encounter roadblocks, and discover shortcuts. After the trip, you review what went well and what you will do differently next time. In other words, you evaluate the trip and get ready for the next one.

Destination

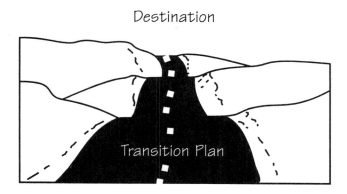

Transition Plan

The following chapters cover each phase of a team transition: Preparing, Mapping, Navigating, and Evaluating. This guidebook brings each phase to life with scenes of team transition successes and setbacks. Checklists and worksheets will guide you through your next trip.

CHAPTER THREE WORKSHEET:
LEARNING FROM PAST TRANSITIONS

Think about the last time your team experienced a change in its membership *(e.g., due to a promotion, transfer, new hire, resignation, leave of absence, retirement, termination, layoff, reorganization, etc.).*

1. How were the roles and responsibilities of the team members coordinated?

_____

_____

_____

_____

_____

_____

2. What was done to prepare all team members for the transition?

_____

_____

_____

_____

_____

_____

3. What was forgotten?

4. How could this team transition have been better prepared, mapped, navigated and evaluated for all parties involved?

5. What specifically will *you* do next time to ensure a more successful team transition?

PHASE ONE:
PREPARING FOR THE TRANSITION

PREPARING

Evaluating — Mapping

Navigating

Many transitions will be new experiences for team members—whether they're entering a new team, leaving a team, or changing their roles. Organizations need to clarify expectations to satisfy interests and control anxieties. Communication—continuous, direct, and open—is the key to successful team transitions.

When preparing for a team transition, it's a good idea to discuss anything and everything you can think of that may be on the minds of the team members affected. Some topics will be sensitive. It's better to discuss it now and openly, rather than later behind others' backs, or not at all.

This chapter contains numerous suggestions for your team as you prepare for your transition. Not all of them will directly apply to your situation. Some ideas, for example, are better used when an organization is downsizing and layoffs are imminent. Others fit best when an organization is growing rapidly and experiencing large-scale hiring and reorganization.

Use this chapter and its lists as a thought-jogger. Feel free to add to the ideas listed.

How To Open Lines Of Communication

During this first phase of a team transition, it's most important to *"keep in touch"*. As a key first step, open lines of communication to clarify goals, needs, interests and expectations, and to open channels for the flow of information.

Give everyone as much accurate information as possible about the upcoming change. They likely have as much vested interest as you do in ensuring that the team transition is successful. This includes sharing a *"We really don't know,"* a *"That's all we have at this time,"* or a *"Here's what we're doing in the meantime"* once in a while. In addition, someone must be available to answer questions and respond to concerns. If not, the rumor mill will take over.

Maintaining a closed-door policy

Rumors are flying . . .

at TypeSet Inc., a typewriter manufacturing plant. Employees sense that devastating cut-backs are on the way. Fears range from major layoffs to plant closure. And management is not available to answer any questions or discuss any suggestions.

Alex, the CEO of this multi-national conglomerate's subsidiary, tried to explain to Louise, the VP of Human Resources, why information about the future of the firm has been scarce.

"We've made a point not to give information to the employees, because there's nothing to share yet," said Alex. *"We really don't know what our parent company is going to do with our product line. I've given them numerous recommendations and they're still being considered. We can't tell employees what we recommended. If some of it got into competitors' hands, we'd be dead. And, what if corporate rejects our proposals? Employees will freak out and lose confidence in us. It's better for us to share nothing until we're sure of it."*

Louise tried her best . . .

to position the employees' concerns.

"Alex, everyone is on edge," she said. *"Our employees aren't stupid. They know the product line is dying. They read it in the paper every day. They follow our sales. They understand the industry. What they don't know is how their management team is responding. And that is what worries them. They need someone to answer their questions and listen to their concerns."*

Alex became impatient. *"Look, I don't have time to pacify them,"* he said. *"This is our problem, not theirs. Just tell everyone to continue business as usual until further notice.". . .*

There are several ways to open lines of communication and clarify employee expectations. Whether you are a manager, a team member, or a Human Resources professional, suggest one or more of the following to be considered during your team transition:

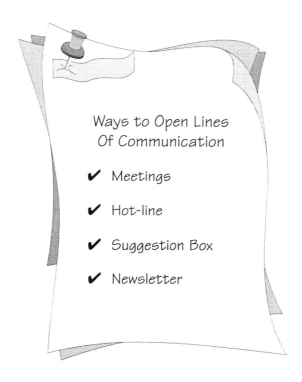

Ways to Open Lines
Of Communication

✔ Meetings

✔ Hot-line

✔ Suggestion Box

✔ Newsletter

Meetings

Schedule regular team meetings to provide information and announce new directions and developments during the transition

period. Allow time for questions and suggestions. Meetings might be organization-wide for general announcements; smaller groups such as team or departmental meetings are more appropriate for two-way communication.

Hot-line

Consider setting up a special telephone line, voice mail or E-mail as a *"hot-line"* to management. Encourage employees to ask questions and share critical information. Assure employees that a credible and respected representative of management will respond to their calls either personally and confidentially, or generally in meetings or a newsletter.

Suggestion Box

The suggestion box is a good vehicle for the open collection and exchange of information, thoughts, and recommendations. It can be an invaluable source of good ideas for team leaders and management during changing times.

Newsletter

Publish a temporary all-employee newsletter. Use it as a vehicle to respond to recurring comments, concerns, ideas, and questions from meetings, the hot-line, suggestion box, rumor mill, or other sources. Call it something like *"Transition Times"*. Remember, the title doesn't have to be fancy, and it *will* be read.

What Expectations To Clarify

Key Questions and Responses

It is difficult if not impossible to anticipate all the information that team members need and want. Each type of change *(e.g., growth, reorganization, downsizing, etc.)* will bring upon teams its own unique set of concerns.

It is, however, critical to anticipate what key questions may arise and the most effective ways to respond to them. When in doubt, ask. And then, ensure that you *(and/or others responsible for fielding these concerns)* are direct, honest, and consistent when answering team members' expectations.

Keeping the door locked

The employees of TypeSet, Inc. suffered . . .

a sudden 15 percent staff reduction. The layoffs were even a surprise to the Human Resources staff who were given only four days warning to administer the whole process. Employees were told to stay in their offices on Friday afternoon until *"someone had a chance to speak to them."* Louise and her HR staff felt like grim reapers.

Employees who survived the initial layoffs asked to be kept in the loop and notified as early as possible if further staffing reductions would be necessary. They received only sporadic responses (*"off the record"*) from a few members of the management team.

Management's actions spoke louder than their words. They decided to further reduce head count by not replacing employees who later resigned or retired within the next six months. This hiring freeze was not announced. The remaining employees were bitter.

Mario, a Production Supervisor, expressed it best. *"We knew there had to be some layoffs,"* he said. *"Our industry is in decline. But the way it was handled . . . all the secrecy, all the surprises. It's insulting. This company will never be the same. They bailed on us. Some of us formerly loyal employees are thinking of doing the same."*

Resignations increased in the following months. Some departments were left in a panic trying to figure out how to handle·the workload with a skeletal staff. Then, the ripple effect took over. Key customers and suppliers, responding to the rumors and grumbles, began questioning the viability of a future for TypeSet Inc.

Don't make the same mistakes. Work with your team to brainstorm the issues that require immediate attention and clarify expectations.

The following lists of expectations to clarify will help you get started. Admittedly, these lists only *"scratch the surface"*.

---

1. Likely questions from all team members experiencing a team transition.

? What is the *"big picture"* for our organization *(e.g., vision, mission, goals, etc.)*?

? How does our team *"fit in"*?

? Why are we going through a team transition?

? What are we hoping to achieve with this change?

? What are our options as a team, and the pros/cons? *(e.g., why couldn't we just stay the way we were?)*

? What will be our new strategic plan *(e.g., objectives, priorities, etc.)*?

? What will be our new operating plan *(e.g., systems, processes, policies, procedures, structures, etc.)*?

? How will each of us be affected?

? What will be our team transition plan? *(e.g., who will be involved, what will we do, and how and when will we do it?)*

? How will we monitor our progress and measure our success during this transition?

? When and how will we get more information?

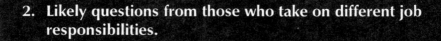
2. Likely questions from those who take on different job responsibilities.

- What will be my new functions, responsibilities, measurements/methods, and reporting relationships?

- What are my options as a team member, and the pros/cons of each? *(e.g., what if I don't agree with the team's plan?)*

- What support will I receive *(e.g., time to learn new skills and tasks, training, equipment, materials, relief, etc.)?*

- Will there be a change in the way my performance is measured *(e.g., expectations, standards, methods of evaluation, etc.)?*

- Will there be a change in compensation or pay grade based on a job reevaluation?

- Will compensation changes be retroactive?

3. Likely questions from those who experience a change in leadership.

- How will this new leader impact our team *(e.g., our strategic and operating plans)?*

- How will this new leader impact my role and responsibilities?

- How will we handle various Human Resources issues in progress *(e.g., performance appraisals, employee relations counseling issues, compensation reviews, job reevaluations, staff recruits, etc.)?*

- What were the selection criteria used for this change in leadership *(promotion, transfer, new employee, etc.)?*

4. Likely questions from those *remaining* team members who experience a change in team membership (*i.e., a reduction or reorganization of staff*).

? How should we consistently respond to direct questions regarding the reason for our reduction or reorganization (*and to whom should we forward more formal requests from the media*)?

? How will we maintain the quality of our services and products?

? How will we keep remaining team members motivated and productive, and avoid getting overloaded or burned-out (*by doing the same amount of work with less or different people*)?

? What other options were considered or are available (*e.g., voluntary layoffs, temporary or part-time status, transfers, salary reductions, temporary plant closures, job-sharing, etc.*)?

? What criteria will be used to determine who goes or stays?

? How will exiting team members be notified?

? How will we keep exiting team members motivated and productive until their last day worked?

? How are exiting team members expected to spend their remaining time with their current team (*see details below*), and what are our options if they don't perform?

? How and for what period of time will we manage the exiting team members' communication (*e.g., responding to customers' direct requests for their services or ways of reaching them, handling their personal telephone calls, voice-mails, E-mails, mail, etc.*)

? How will we maintain security and confidentiality during this transition (*e.g., accounting for company property and proprietary information, enforcing security clearances, etc.*).

(continued on next page)

4. Likely questions from those *remaining* team members who experience a change in team membership *(i.e., a reduction or reorganization of staff)—continued.*

? How will the team manage future visitations by exiting team members?

? Will there be a change in hiring practices *(e.g., a hiring freeze)?*

? If we experience unanticipated staff turnover *(e.g., resignations)*, will these positions be replaced?

? If there are layoffs, are they permanent?

? Will there be a chance of a recall, and if so, what are the procedures?

? What are our policies and procedures on letters of recommendation, reference checks, etc.

? How should we *"bid farewell"* to exiting team members? For example:
- determining and respecting their interests in ways to part with remaining team members
- combining efforts, if preferable, with other exiting members *(e.g., a larger party)*
- scheduling activities to avoid conflicts with business operations
- managing expenses

? Will there be more reductions in staff?

? What are the indicators to monitor for such a decision?

? What are our plans to avoid or minimize the possibility of this happening again?

(Also see # 5 below—there will be an overlap in interests between remaining and exiting employees).

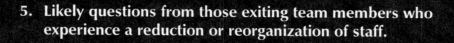
5. Likely questions from those exiting team members who experience a reduction or reorganization of staff.

- What were the decision criteria and process to determine who goes and who stays?

- Will exiting team members receive notice and/or severance pay?

- How will benefits be affected?

- Will there be consideration of rehire or transfers?

- What is the process for re-applying for other job openings should they arise in the future?

- Will time-off-with-pay be provided for existing employees to interview for other jobs before leaving?

- Will there be exit interviews?

- Will employment references and letters of recommendation be provided upon request?

- Will out placement training and/or job placement services be available?

- When and for how long will there be access to offices before and after the exiting team members' last days worked (*e.g., work spaces, telephones, voice mail, files, personal computers, E-mail, fax machines, copiers, staff support, etc.*)?

(*continued on next page*)

5. Likely questions from those exiting team members who experience a reduction or reorganization of staff.
　—continued

? How are exiting team members expected to spend their remaining time with their current team? For example:

- completing portions of the Team Transition Worksheet *(see Chapters Five and Six)*
- documenting procedures essential for continuous and smooth team operations
- cross-training others who assume the responsibilities of departing employees
- reviewing computer database directories and passwords with others
- informing customers, suppliers, and contacts of their new status, how to reach them in the future, and who is taking over their responsibilities *(as deemed necessary and desirable by the remaining team members)*
- transferring memberships to professional organizations
- changing mailing addresses for personal mail and newsletters
- closing out expense reports
- resolving the status of company reimbursements *(e.g., travel, tuition, etc.)*
- returning all company property
- discussing post-employment contact *(ways for others to contact existing employees for questions, advice, etc.)*

(Also see # 4 above—there will be an overlap in interests between remaining and existing employees).

Treating employees as valued resources

Another typewriter manufacturer, KeyStrokes Inc., . . .

handled the same market decline in a completely different way. Employees at this plant requested open and accurate information, which they received

through a newsletter and quarterly all-employee meetings. The President, LeAnne, didn't hold back or give up as she laid it all on the line to her employees.

LeAnne discussed the declining market shares, the proposals to streamline operations, and the move to diversify—

possibly toward more sophisticated circuit boards. She also shared the market and budget conditions under which tough decisions like staff reductions would have to be made. And they were tough—the work force was reduced by twelve percent in the next quarter. . . .

"It was and always will be *our last resort*," LeAnne explained at the last meeting. *"Fortunately, we were able to achieve our short-term goals to immediately reduce our operating budget. Credit is largely due to the early retirement and volunteer separation programs Human Resources designed in the past few months. Only four percent of our team was involuntary laid off. And we are working closely with these employees to ease their transitions to other jobs."*

"In the meantime," she said. *"I'm open to any and all means to continue to turn this situation around. I don't have all the answers, but together we will find them.".* .

LeAnne minimized anxiety and confusion because she made the employees feel that they were getting the whole story. Exiting team members felt they were treated fairly and respectfully. They were actively involved with remaining team members to orchestrate a smooth team transition.

It wasn't fun or enjoyable. In fact, the process of letting productive employees go was quite emotional. But, it was handled professionally.

In the subsequent months, remaining employees stepped forward with suggestions *(including innovative ways to further cut operating costs and waste)*. Everyone pitched in to keep overhead to a minimum. This bought time for the management team to determine the next steps for a more promising future.

Chapter Four Worksheet:
Clarifying Expectations

Prepare for an upcoming transition where members will be exiting your team *(e.g., due to a layoff, reorganization, promotion, transfer, resignation, leave of absence, retirement, termination, etc.).* Note your initial responses to each question in the worksheet that follows.

Feel free to add to this worksheet later following a discussion with your team.

1. How can others in your organization open the lines of communication with you and your team about the organization's transition?

2. How can you and your team open the lines of communication with others about your team's transition?

3. In addition to the expectations listed in this chapter from *remaining* members who experience a change in team membership *(a reduction or a reorganization in staff),* what other expectations need clarification?

4. Describe ways for you, your team and/or other leaders to clarify these additional expectations of *remaining* members.

5. In addition to the expectations listed in this chapter from *exiting* members who experience a change in team membership *(a reduction or a reorganization in staff),* what other expectations need clarification?

6. Describe ways for you, your team, and/or other leaders to clarify these additional expectations of *exiting* members.

CLARIFYING EXPECTATIONS

1. How Others Can Open Communication Lines	2. How You/Your Team Can Open Communcation Lines
3. Additional Expectations of *Remaining* Members	4. Ways To Clarify
5. Additional Expectations of *Exiting* Members	6. Ways To Clarify

PHASE TWO:
MAPPING THE TRANSITION

"I was seldom to see an opportunity

until it had ceased to be one."

Mark Twain

Ever take off on a trip without a map? It's OK for a simple joy ride. It allows for a bit of spontaneity. Who cares where you end up or how you got there? Have some fun. There's nothing wrong with that. But when it comes to organization team transitions, it's not a good idea.

When To Consider Mapping An Approach

What if you're on a business trip and need to arrive at a particular place at a particular time? Others are counting on you *(like those coworkers in the back seat)* and you have limited fuel.

You need to consider mapping an approach for the best way to get there. If not, you could be taking on more than a fair share of risk.

What if you make a wrong turn? What if you run into bad weather? Poor road conditions? A dead end? You can also drive right by an important site to see, or a shortcut you didn't know was there.

Preparing

Evaluating ——— MAPPING

Navigating

Sure, road signs along the way will help you, and you can always regroup at the next rest stop. But you can't see what's on the other side of the mountain until you've gone around it. And then it's too late.

You're then told about easier ways to get to where you wanted to go. An alternative route through a mountain pass, a train that tunnels through the center of the range, a cheap plane ride that jumps over to your final destination.

The suggestions come from those who have traveled this land before. Those with experience. Those with a map—a worksheet of options to destinations.

"Thanks. I'll remember that next time," you sarcastically mutter. Well, now *is* the next time.

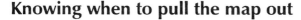
Knowing when to pull the map out

Alan has just been hired . . .

along with several others, by PSYCO, a small, growing organization that produces high-end comic books, pogs, and stickers. It is a very exciting time. Everyone has high energy and is doing anything and everything possible to meet the demands of the competitive marketplace. Promotions are frequent and team membership is continually changing.

Although Alan is thrilled about his new analyst position, he is also very concerned. Many employees have expressed feelings of burn-out. A coworker, Del, summed it up. *"It seems like we're constantly reinventing the wheel around here,"* he said, *"or spinning them out of control. We're stepping on each others' toes. Going in fifteen directions at once. It's exhilarating, though—no question about it."*

"But it's beginning to take its toll in stressed-out workers, excessive overtime, rising inefficiencies, duplications of effort, commitments slipping through the cracks, increases in rework and waste," he continued. *"Even though we're raking in the dough, the costs could catch up with us."*

"By now, we're starting to see the right ways of doing things," said Del. *"We need to regroup and clarify our roles and responsibilities. Tighten-up a few systems, policies, and processes that are in flux."*

Alan and Del sense it's time for a map—a way to chart the best course of action for this team transition. Alan looks at this as a golden opportunity to make an immediate, positive impact on his team.

Passing a map over to the next driver

Shirley is in charge . . .

of Public Relations at WaterWorks, a local utilities company. She has accepted a position with another organization and will be leaving in two weeks. Shirley has been in her present position for six years. In that time, she has gradually reshaped her original role and approach. For instance, she learned that her time was much better spent addressing her customers' needs *"informally and live"* during field visits, rather than by making telephone calls or scheduling formal business luncheons.

Everyone agrees that Shirley has done a terrific job with Public Relations. No one has recorded her improved methods and priorities. In addition, no one knows the status of media communication regarding the new utilities project affecting many residential customers.

The organization was fortunate. Shirley took the initiative to record her job responsibilities and priorities. She also noted the progress of critical communication projects, and suggestions to make the job more efficient in the future.

Not all team members, however, are as assertive and conscientious as Shirley. Organizations must have a systematic way to map team transitions.

How To Use A Team Transition Worksheet

The Team Transition Worksheet in this chapter is a proven format that will enable your team to map its course toward a successful transition.

By mapping out the transition, you will avoid pitfalls and seize opportunities. Use each of the considerations provided in the Team Transition Worksheet as a starting point. Feel free to customize the worksheet based on your own needs.

Let's review the Team Transition Worksheet.

TEAM TRANSITION WORKSHEET

Team: _____
Member: _____

Role/Position: _____

Page: _____
Date: _____

PRESENT PERFORMANCE RECORD

Key Functions	Key Responsibilities	Key Measurements & Methods

PROGRESS REPORT

(Optional)

FUTURE TRANSITION PLAN

Potentially Negotiable Components	Core Needs & Filters	Negotiated Changes (Eliminate, Reshape, Reassign)	Required Actions	Targeted Results (Savings, Impacts, Etc.)

What is the purpose?

Use this Team Transition Worksheet to plan, document, and evaluate the activities involved in a team transition. It facilitates an essential discussion of all responsibilities and tasks of all team members—whether they're entering, remaining, or exiting.

This process will help you determine the most effective and efficient way to reallocate your team's resources (*e.g., time, systems and procedures, materials, equipment, money, etc.*) to successfully support changing priorities.

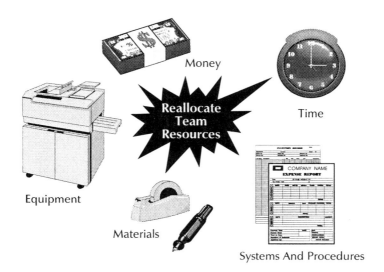

What are the benefits?

The worksheet involves all team members. It defines who's going to do what—and new ways of doing it. It helps teams gain clearer communication and understanding. It challenges performance expectations and prompts your team to share them. It helps you redirect your team's efforts to address new strategic priorities, customer requirements, and operating constraints.

Planning also helps team members avoid unnecessary fire-fighting, things *"slipping through the cracks,"* poor allocation of resources (*e.g., getting overloaded with work after a reduction in staff*), duplication of efforts, inefficient activities, and overlooked opportunities.

How is it designed?

The worksheet is divided into three sections:

On the left side are spaces to list *"who is doing what"* before a team transition—the Present Performance Record. In the center is a column to register the status of special projects and assignments. On the right side are columns to record negotiated changes and actions required for transitioning these responsibilities.

Think of the worksheet as a bridge. On the left, or the beginning of the bridge, record what is *happening (Present Performance Record).* In the center of the bridge, record where things stand *(Progress Report).* On the right side, record where you're going and how you're getting there *(Future Transition Plan).*

When should you use it?

Once your team is aware it will go through a transition, bring out the worksheet! Continue to use the worksheet during *and* after a team transition.

Team transitions occur in response to changes in strategic business focus, operating plans, roles, and responsibilities; or priorities due to organizational growth, downsizing, turnover in team membership or leadership, reorganizations, and mergers or acquisitions.

Who should complete it?

All team members, both remaining and exiting, as well as the team leader, share the responsibility for completing the Team Transition

Worksheet. By tapping into all of your creative resources, you and your team will identify better ways to achieve your new goals.

Each individual should complete the Present Performance Record and Progress Report first. Then the team should discuss each worksheet together and complete the Future Transition Plan.

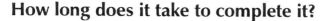
How long does it take to complete it?

First drafts for individuals may take 30 minutes to one hour. Then, it may take the team one to two hours to complete each worksheet together.

Consider this time an investment that will pay big dividends. For example, a team of six may take six to 12 hours to redirect it's critical activities for the next year. This up-front investment could save lots of time that would have been wasted by an unfocused work team. This also helps you avoid or minimize losses suffered from turnover, low morale, burn-out, and decreased productivity.

Is it mandatory to use it?

No and yes. Using *this* particular Team Transition Worksheet *is not* mandatory. It is simply provided as a tool that captures a critical

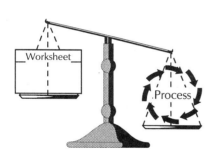

negotiation process you should consider during a team transition. Feel free to adapt and expand this form to meet your team's particular needs and preferences. Or, use it as a visual guide to structure your own worksheet and group's discussions (*i.e., it's not the form that is important, it's the process!*).

The process of reevaluating how to allocate team resources by discussing negotiable components of responsibilities *is* mandatory if a team wants to reach its greatest potential during changing times.

Is there anything to be wary of?

Yes. For example, some team leaders may use this Team Transition Worksheet to identify and reassign *only* the responsibilities of a member who is leaving a group.

Such team leaders make many unrealistic assumptions. First, that the remaining team members must take on the exiting member's work *"as is"* on top of their full loads. The outcome is often overworked and frustrated employees.

Team leaders and members could avoid this typical crash-and-burn scenario by taking a moment to quickly review what's currently on their plates and eliminate or reshape a few tasks if possible. This helps team members make room for any additional priorities allocated from the departing member.

Note: Chapter Six covers several other cautions and pitfalls.

How To Complete The Worksheet

Following is an overview of the process for completing the Team Transition Worksheet.

Present Performance Record

Before a team transition occurs, have each exiting and remaining team member complete a Present Performance Record—a list of Key Functions, Key Responsibilities, and Key Measurements and Methods.

TEAM TRANSITION WORKSHEET								
PRESENT PERFORMANCE RECORD			PROGRESS REPORT	FUTURE TRANSITION PLAN				
Key Functions	Key Responsibilities	Key Measurements & Methods	(Optional)	Essential Negotiable Components	Core Needs & Fluids	Negotiated Changes (Eliminate, Reshape, Reassign)	Required Actions	Targeted Results (Savings, Impacts, Etc.)

Key Functions

List the four to seven key functions of your job. Identify *(or label)* them in phrases.

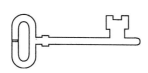

For example, when you move from one house to another, you box all of your personal belongings and label each box "Kitchen," "Master Bedroom," etc. Now imagine that you are about to move from one job to another and have to put all of your responsibilities into five to seven boxes. How would you label them? These labels are your key functions.

Key Responsibilities

For each key function, list three to six key responsibilities for which you are held accountable. This list may include tasks you complete

on a regular basis as well as special projects that you must complete within a particular time frame.

"Key" means critical, essential . . . *big!* The tasks that are most important need to be addressed the quickest, etc. Yes, you likely do *much more,* but try to limit your list to the most critical priorities and objectives that are *worthy of discussion with your team at this time. (The other less important tasks and to-do's can be addressed at a later time—with or without the entire team—within another week, month, etc. Often decisions can be made quickly by an individual or two later. It's important not to get bogged down in the details at the start.)*

Key Measurements And Methods

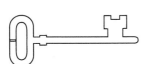

For each key responsibility, list one to three key ways your performance is measured. Identify *what* is measured and *how* it is measured.

Note: You may find this list repetitive—some measurements and methods may assess many responsibilities. If this is the case, don't worry about a one-for-one connection of measurements with responsibilities. Your list of two to three measurements and methods will better match up with the 0more general key function within the same row of the worksheet.

Progress Report *(Optional)*

Have each exiting and remaining team member complete a Progress Report, as necessary, for any key responsibilities that are project-oriented. These tend to be special projects, assignments, or tasks that must be completed within a particular timeframe *(e.g., design a new form, create a procedure, install a system, initiate a report, commence a project, etc)*.

TEAM TRANSITION WORKSHEET								
Team: _____ Member: _____			Role Position: _____			Page: _____ Date: _____		
PRESENT PERFORMANCE RECORD			PROGRESS REPORT	FUTURE TRANSITION PLAN				
Key Functions	Key Responsibilities	Key Requirements & Methods	(Optional)	Potential; Negotiable Components	Core Needs & Fixes	Negotiated Changes (Eliminate, Reshape, Reassign)	Required Actions	Targeted Results (Savings, Impacts, Etc.)

The Progress Report should identify how far along the project is at the time of the team transition, what are the next steps toward completion, and where further information can be found. In some cases, it may be helpful to add *"editorial comments"* such as whether or not the project should be completed as previously planned and why or why not.

Note: This progress report section is *optional*. It is not necessary for addressing ongoing tasks and recurring responsibilities *(e.g., answering customer service calls on a daily basis)*, yet it's often necessary for tracking the status of specific projects *(e.g., following up on the Penske file)*.

Future Transition Plan

As a team, examine the key functions, responsibilities, measurements, and methods that all team members listed in their Present Performance Records. Also, check the current status of special projects and assignments that they listed in their optional Progress Reports.

Then, look for ways to streamline tasks to save time and money in the future. Optimize the use of your team's resources!

TEAM TRANSITION WORKSHEET

Team: _____ Page: _____
Member: _____ Role/Position: _____ Date: _____

PRESENT PERFORMANCE RECORD			PROGRESS REPORT	FUTURE TRANSITION PLAN				
Key Functions	Key Responsibilities	Key Measurements & Methods	(Optional)	Potentially Negotiable Components	Core Needs & Filters	Negotiated Changes (Eliminate, Reshape, Reassign)	Required Actions	Targeted Results (Savings, Impacts, Etc.)

Potentially Negotiable Components

As a team, discuss and finalize the Potentially Negotiable Components section of the worksheet, *and* complete the rest of the Future Transition Plan as described below.

Note: Determine whether or not to include exiting employees in these discussions before they leave. They are often eager to help the team continue to be successful after they leave. As a minimum, have each exiting and remaining team member individually begin to complete the Potentially Negotiable Components section of the Future Transition Plan. Use their initial notes as a *"kick start"* for a future team meeting. You will find more details about this step in Chapter Six.

For example, brainstorm potentially negotiable components of key responsibilities of a given task. Ask, *"What can we reshape or change about the task before reassigning it to someone else?" "Can we do it less often?" "Can we make it less complex or time-consuming?" "Can we give it to someone else?"* Jot all ideas on the worksheet or a separate sheet of paper.

This listing will eventually help you avoid the trap of unrealistically reassigning work *"as is"* to remaining team members with full loads. A partial list of potentially negotiable components of projects and tasks follows. A more extensive list is available in the Appendix.

POTENTIALLY NEGOTIABLE COMPONENTS

➢ Accuracy

➢ Availability

➢ Cost

➢ Frequency

➢ Format

➢ Quantity

➢ Timeliness

➢ Thoroughness

Exiting employees may have some excellent suggestions for eliminating or reshaping their tasks *(since they have everything to gain from maintaining a favorable reputation in the business world).*

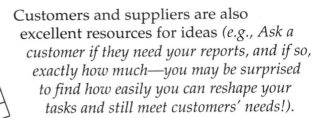

Use Each Team Member To Gain A Strategic Advantage

Customers and suppliers are also excellent resources for ideas *(e.g., Ask a customer if they need your reports, and if so, exactly how much—you may be surprised to find how easily you can reshape your tasks and still meet customers' needs!).*

Remaining team members may already feel overburdened and anxious about the unknown future. This process will open discussions on the values, needs, and expectations of all responsibilities before making future commitments. Recognize that even if a task is reassigned *"as is"* after all the analysis, the receiver will know exactly *why* it must be done.

Core Needs And Filters

Now you need to determine what *"filters"* you will use to help you choose what to do with each responsibility. You want to make sure, for example, that if you reshape a task, it will still meet critical customer needs! Possible *"filters"* include, but are not limited to:

➠ Alignment with core customer needs.

➠ Alignment with your organization's strategic vision, mission, and goals.

➠ Alignment with your team's strategic objectives and priorities.

➠ Compliance with mandates and requirements from government or legal entities, management, etc.

➠ Feasibility given resource constraints *(i.e., the amount of time, effort, training, skills, equipment, money, etc., needed to implement the Negotiated Changes).*

Negotiated Changes

Considering these *"filters,"* make one of the following team decisions *(listed in recommended order of consideration):*

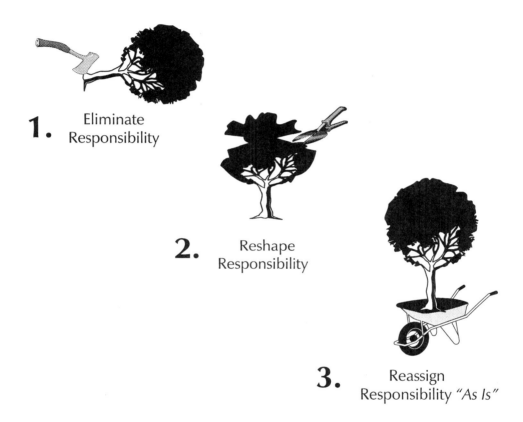

1. Eliminate
Responsibility

2. Reshape
Responsibility

3. Reassign
Responsibility *"As Is"*

Continue this process for each key responsibility. Decide and note in the Negotiated Changes section of the worksheet *one* of the team decisions above.

Note: When you choose *"Reshape,"* remember to also list the negotiable components of the task that are to be reshaped before the responsibility is reassigned. This will likely be a *"short list"* taken from the Potentially Negotiable Components column.

Required Actions

As a team, determine and note *"who will need to do what, when, and how"* to eliminate, reshape, or reassign *"as is."*

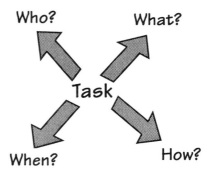

Who? What?

Task

When? How?

When you eliminate a responsibility:

☑ Notify all internal and external customers and suppliers that you will no longer handle this responsibility.

☑ Offer alternatives *when possible* to meet their needs.

When you reshape a responsibility:

☑ Ensure that you rechecked the core need behind the task.

☑ Ensure that you used the core need to filter the potentially negotiable components and reshape the responsibility into its most efficient and effective form.

☑ Reassign the reshaped responsibility to a remaining team member, another team, etc.

☑ Notify all internal and external customers and suppliers of the reassignment

☑ Determine when and how you will make the changes to reshape the responsibility before it is reassigned.

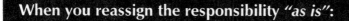
When you reassign the responsibility *"as is"*:

☑ Ensure that the task is in its most efficient and effective form to meet the core need.

☑ Or, verify that the responsibility is directly meeting a strict legal requirement and there is no possibility of changing it.

☑ Determine whether you can reassign it to another team member or team.

☑ Notify all internal and external customers of the reassignment only if a different team member receives it.

When you reassign a responsibility *(regardless of whether or not you reshape it)*, consider the following:

⑨ Will the member receiving the assigned responsibility require *"start-up"* time *(or training or other resources)* to learn to complete the task?

⑨ Could the reassigning of this responsibility imply that the member receiving it has *"free time"* to handle it?

⑨ If not, what responsibility currently on his/her plate will you eliminate or reshape to allow time for the successful completion of this new responsibility?

⑨ How will you ensure that the member receiving the reassigned responsibility will be successful and not overburdened?

When you make *any* decision whatsoever, consider the following:

- Why wasn't this done before?

- Why will it be successful *now?*

- Have you included those who will be affected by the implementation in the creation of your Future Transition Plan?

- How will your team evaluate the progress of this required action plan?

Targeted Results

As a team, discuss and establish Targeted Results—goals you will strive to achieve with the implementation of the Future Transition Plan. Consider the following:

 What is the new projected time to complete the reshaped/reassigned responsibility?

 What is the estimated time savings per day, week, month, etc., based on the elimination or reshaping of the responsibility?

 What other savings will your team gain?

 What costs will you incur?

You can often use this section to help *"sell"* the elimination or reshaping of a responsibility *(e.g., management and customers like to hear about various savings)*. You can also use it to keep track of how much is on each person's plate *(e.g., add up all of the new projected times to complete each responsibility and compare the sum to a 40 or 50-hour workweek)*. This process will ensure no one is under-utilized or overburdened.

"Teaming Up" During A Transition

Refer to the following as an example of how the Team Transition Summary can be used on the job. Remember, this is only an illustration. Your team will come up with hundreds of variations as it reevaluates how to reallocate team resources during changing times.

CompuTeach, Inc., a manufacturer . . .

of educational software with 80 employees, has undergone a reorganization to better align itself with changing market needs. More emphasis will be placed on opening new markets, research and development, and technical support *(servicing end users' calls and providing user-friendly reference manuals)*; less will be placed on supplemental product lines and training services. The company took all of the necessary steps to keep lines of communication open and to manage employees expectations. *(See Chapter Four.)*

TSS Team

Member 1
Member 5
Member 2
Member 6
Member 3
Member 7
Member 4
Member 8

One Division of the company, Training Services and Support *(TSS)*, will transfer three of its eight employees to other functions within the next month. The team may further reduce in size over the next year and a half—all employees will be working with the Human Resources staff to look for new opportunities within CompuTeach as the company continues to grow.

Although everyone is excited and supportive of the changes, the remaining five employees are concerned about how they will continue to service their customers after about a 40% cut in the Division's staff. . . .

TSS was established . . .

as a profit center to offer direct training and consulting support to end users, above and beyond the reference manuals provided with their software. TSS offers regular public training workshops and seminars for beginners to experts in 24 major markets around the nation. Interested users simply sign up to attend the seminar of their choice and learn more about the software they have purchased. TSS also provides off-the-shelf training programs and consulting support to corporate clients. To supplement the software reference guides, TSS also has its own mini-product line of training booklets that illustrate complex applications. The booklets are shipped to order. Although the Division was relatively successful in paying for itself, the owners decided there was more money in products than in these services.

A quick look at the TSS Division organization chart, employees, and key functions follows. . . .

TSS Division

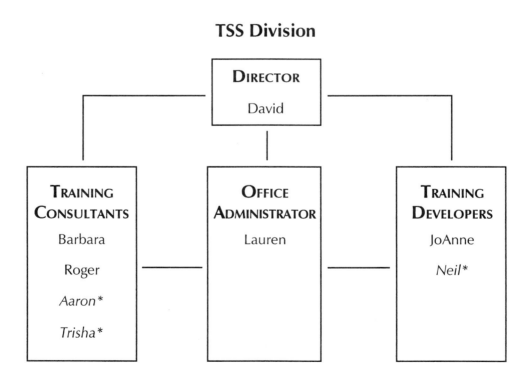

*Leaving the TSS Division in one month

Roger approached David . . .

and asked if it would be OK for the team to use the Team Transition Worksheet to assist David with this organizational change, and sold the idea *(using this guidebook!)*. David agreed to review the process in a staff meeting the next day. Roger gave a brief training session on the purpose and use of the Team Transition Worksheet. David asked everyone to complete the Present Performance Record and Progress Report sections of the worksheet within a few days. To help everyone with a successful *"kick-start,"* the team decided to use a portion of this meeting to brainstorm everyone's Key Functions. Their rough notes follow. . . .

TSS KEY FUNCTIONS				
Role/ Position	**Director**	**Training Consultants**	**Training Developers**	**Office Administrator**
Key Functions	✓ Strategic planning	▪ Program sales	→ Product sales	❖ Program contract administration
	✓ Sales management	▪ Program scheduling & enrollment	→ Product research	❖ Product sales administration
	✓ Operations management	▪ Program delivery	→ Product design & development	❖ Reception & office administration
	✓ Marketing/ advertising	▪ Program evaluation	→ General administration	
	✓ Finance/ budgeting	▪ General consulting & customer service		
	✓ Supervising (staffing, compensation, performance appraisal, etc.)	▪ General administration		
	✓ General administration			

Note: No two individuals or teams will *"label"* their responsibilities with the same *"functions"*—they may use different words to describe the function or organize the responsibilities into different groupings that represent a different function. This is fine. The discussion will be healthy, and the wording isn't important. What is important is for everyone to eventually agree that the Key Responsibilities of the team are captured one place or another so that they are not overlooked in upcoming discussions.

TEAM TRANSITION WORKSHEET								
Team: _____ Member: _____				Role Position: _____		Page: _____ Date: _____		
PRESENT PERFORMANCE RECORD			PROGRESS REPORT	FUTURE TRANSITION PLAN				
Key Functions	Key Responsibilities	Key Measurements & Methods	(Optional)	Potential/ Negotiable Competence	Core Needs & Gives	Negotiated Changes (Eliminate, Reshape, Reassign)	Required Actions	Targeted Results (Results Savings, Impacts, Etc.)

Everyone then took . . .

this list and fleshed out a Present Performance Record and Progress Report. As an example, Lauren's worksheets follow. . . .

TEAM TRANSITION WORKSH

Team: TSS

Member: Lauren Mark

Role/Position: Office Admi

PRESENT PERFORMANCE RECORD			PROGRESS REPORT		
Key Functions	Key Responsibilities	Key Measurements & Methods	(Optional)	Potentially Negotiable Components	Core Nee & Filters
Program contract administration.	Process and coordinate proposals and contracts.	Accuracy and timeliness of typing, distributing, filing per Training Consultants requirements.	Two proposals and five contracts are pending processing.		
	Coordinate program training site arrangements.	Diplomatic and efficient per customer feedback.	Six scheduled public seminars, need arrangements.		
	Monitor contract expenses.	Organized, accurate, and in compliance with contract and policy guidelines.	Two customer complaints of discrepancies need follow-up.		
	Coordinate travel arrangements.	Compliance with contract, customer, and Training Coordinator requirements.	Six major public seminars need travel arrangements for Training Consultants.		
	Special project: Assist Training Consultants with reformatting and automating of the Contract-In-Progress report.	Achieve project objectives per plan.	Have not started.		

TEAM TRANSITION WORKSH

Team: TSS

Member: Lauren Mark

Role/Position: Office Admi

	PRESENT PERFORMANCE RECORD		PROGRESS REPORT		
Key Functions	Key Responsibilities	Key Measurements & Methods	*(Optional)*	Potentially Negotiable Components	Core Nee & Filters
Product sales administration.	Receive and process all product orders (by phone, fax and mail).	Efficient and accurate handling per customer feedback.	Order fulfillment is current.		
	Prepare and direct shipments.	Efficient and cost effective.	Not Applicable. (N/A)		
	Monitor and report inventories.	Accuracy and timeliness.	N/A		
	Special project: Reformat and update program and product/service catalog by XX/XX/XX.	Accuracy, thoroughness, ease of reference, and effectiveness per customer requirements.	Have not started.		

TEAM TRANSITION WORKSH

Team: TSS

Member: Lauren Mark

Role/Position: Office Admi

PRESENT PERFORMANCE RECORD			PROGRESS REPORT		
Key Functions	Key Responsibilities	Key Measurements & Methods	(Optional)	Potentially Negotiable Components	Core Nee & Filters
Reception and office administration.	Answer, screen and direct telephone calls.	Pleasant greeting within three rings and efficient handling per customer feedback.	N/A		
	Greet, screen and direct office visitors.	Professional bearing, thorough knowledge to accurately and efficiently direct visitors per customer feedback.	N/A		
	Take and deliver messages.	Timely, accurate, legible and complete.	N/A		
	Special project: Assist Director with mass mailing of marketing materials by XX/XX/XX.	Achieve project objectives per plan.	64 of 1000 done; production standards too high or understaffed.		
	Special project: Assist Training Consultants to automate program enrollment process by XX/XX/XX.	Achieve project objectives per plan.	Participated in two meetings; volunteered to research software on the market.		

Note: Lauren's worksheet does not include all of the details—just enough words to capture the essential data per column. (*Remember, this is a worksheet to generate discussion, not a final will and testament!*) Lauren's worksheet also doesn't represent every single thing she does—just the critical responsibilities and projects that must be discussed as a team now. Her other minor *"to-do's"* (*monitoring supplies, receiving, logging and directing periodic deliveries, assisting with new hire orientations, coordinating the year-end party, etc.*) can be covered with the team or by herself and/or a colleague at a later date.

TEAM TRANSITION WORKSHEET								
Team: _____						Page: _____		
Member: _____			Role/Position: _____			Date: _____		
PRESENT PERFORMANCE RECORD			PROGRESS REPORT	FUTURE TRANSITION PLAN				
Key Functions	Key Responsibilities	Key Measurements & Methods	(Optional)	Potentially Negotiable Components	Core Needs & Filters	Negotiated Changes (Eliminate, Reshape, Reassign)	Required Actions	Targeted Results (Savings, Impacts, Etc.)

Once everyone had . . .

their Present Performance Records and Progress reports completed, David scheduled a team meeting to begin to determine the Future Transition Plan. Everyone agreed it would be a good idea to include the exiting employees—Aaron, Trisha and Neil. Barbara was nominated to facilitate the meeting, and JoAnne agreed to be the recorder.

The meeting began. David asked everyone to set their worksheets on the conference table and to step back. *"Look around the room,"* he stated. *"Three of the eight of us won't be here in a month. And on the table is enough work to keep eight people challenged full time. Obviously, something has to change. Our job today is to look at each of our past responsibilities with fresh eyes. Forget for a moment who used to do what, how, and when. Instead, we need to refocus on why—and determine the best way to reallocate our resources to meet our new goals and objectives while we keep our customers happy. Barbara has agreed to help us through this process."*. . .

Barbara stepped forward . . .

"We're going to begin by discussing each of these worksheets one at a time. Our objective is to begin to draft Future Transition Plans together on each worksheet. JoAnne will document our ideas directly on these worksheets." Barbara proceeded to explain the purpose and use of this portion of the worksheet. Then she summarized, *"After this initial discussion, we'll need to go back and review, revise, and agree to a Team Transition Plan. This will likely take several meetings over the next two to three weeks—and nothing will be put in concrete. David has agreed that we can always reshape our plans along the way as we learn more from our experiences."* The team looked ready . . .

"Let's begin with Lauren's worksheets. Lauren, please give us an overview of your Present Performance Record and Progress Report, one function and responsibility at a time. The rest of us are free to ask questions to ensure we understand each Key Responsibility. Then, I'll facilitate a group discussion on Potentially Negotiable Components, Core Needs and Filters, etc. for each Key Responsibility. We'll all need to equally participate in this discussion. Remember, this is not Lauren's problem—it's a challenge to our team to figure out what best to do. Together we can discover new ways to achieve our goals and leverage our talent. As a matter of fact, some of the most creative and objective ideas may come from those of us least familiar with the responsibilities being discussed!"

Lauren began and the team quickly chimed in. Some of the results of their initial discussions follow. These are excerpts from two of the original worksheets submitted by each employee. The ideas generated from the team were noted by JoAnne directly in the Future Transition Plan sections of each worksheet. . . .

TEAM TRANSITION

Team: TSS

Member: Lauren Mark

PRESENT PERFORMANCE RECORD			PROGRESS REPORT
Key Functions	Key Responsibilities	Key Measurements & Methods	(Optional)
Program contract administration.	Process and coordinate proposals and contracts.	Accuracy and timeliness of typing, distributing, filing per Training Consultants requirements.	Two proposals and five contracts are pending processing.
	Special project: Assist Training Consultants with reformatting and automating of the Contract-in-Progress report.	Achieve project objectives per plan.	Have not started.
Product sales administration.	Receive and process all product orders (by phone, fax and mail).	Efficient and accurate handling per customer feedback.	Order fulfillment is current.
	Monitor and report inventories.	Accuracy and timeliness.	N/A

WORKSHEET

Role/Position:	Office Administrator	Page:	X of X (excerpt)
		Date:	10-1-XX

FUTURE TRANSITION PLAN

Potentially Negotiable Components	Core Needs & Filters	Negotiated Changes (Eliminate, Reshape, Reassign)	Required Actions	Targeted Results (Savings, Impacts, Etc.)
Accuracy. Timeliness. Scope. Consistency. Ease of reference. Contract clauses and amendments. Staffing. Procedures.	Alignment with customer need for accuracy per negotiated agreements with Consultants.	**Reshape and reassign** to Consultants. (Consultants do their own proposals and contracts directly on computer templates.)	Create templates on system file server by XX/XX/XX. Train the Consultants by XX/XX/XX.	Decrease to 0 hrs per week (10 hours savings for Administrator and one hour per week addition for Consultants for proofing and distributing.)
Objectives. Necessity. Dimension. Format. Availability. Frequency.	Alignment with Director's need for data for management report.	**Eliminate.** (Information will be automatically available on-line after proposal and contract processing is on file server.)	Train Director how to access information by XX/XX/XX.	Decrease to 0 hours in the next month (6-8 hours savings).
Accuracy. Frequency. Responsiveness. Schedule.	Alignment with customer need to place orders at the time of their call, and receive shipments within month.	**Reshape.** (Use voice mail system for automated order taking. Process orders once per week vs. daily. Emphasize use of fax and mail in marketing.)	Upgrade voice mail system and message prompts by XX/XX/XX. Change marketing materials by XX/XX/XX.	Decrease to 6 hours per week (2 hours savings).
Accuracy. Timeliness. Availability. Currency. Dimension. Frequency.	Alignment with Director's need for data for management report.	**Reshape.** (Put inventories on-line to be available as needed.)	Transfer raw inventory data to file server by by XX/XX/XX. Train Director how to access information by XX/XX/XX.	Decrease to 0 hours per month (4 hours savings).

TEAM TRANSITION

Team: TSS

Member: Lauren Mark

PRESENT PERFORMANCE RECORD			PROGRESS REPORT
Key Functions	Key Responsibilities	Key Measurements & Methods	*(Optional)*
Product sales administration. *(continued)*	Special project: Reformat and update program and product/service catalog by XX/XX/XX.	Accuracy, thoroughness, ease of reference, and effectiveness per customer requirements.	Have not started.
Reception and office administration.	Special project: Assist Director with mass mailing of marketing materials by XX/XX/XX.	Achieve project objectives per plan.	64 of 1000 done; production standards too high or understaffed.
	Special project: Assist Training Consultants to automate program enrollment process by XX/XX/XX.	Achieve project objectives per plan.	Participated in two meetings; volunteered to research software on the market.

WORKSHEET

Page: X of X (excerpt)

Role/Position: Office Administrator

Date: 10-1-XX

FUTURE TRANSITION PLAN

Potentially Negotiable Components	Core Needs & Filters	Negotiated Changes (Eliminate, Reshape, Reassign)	Required Actions	Targeted Results (Savings, Impacts, Etc.)
Accuracy. Thoroughness. Ease of reference. Effectiveness per customer requirements. Delivery schedule. Necessity. Format. Costs.	Alignment with customer need for some reference for ordering (current catalog has worked fine).	**Eliminate.** (Use current catalog until supplies are depleted.)	Notify the big boss about this change by XX/XX/XX.	Decrease to 0 hours in the next month (60-80 hours savings, and $12,000 savings in printing and distributing costs).
Objectives. Standards. Necessity. Quantity. Staffing. Schedule.	Alignment with company goals and new budget constraints.	**Reshape and Reassign** to external source. (Reduce mailing to 500.)	Reduce mailing list by XX/XX/XX. Secure contract with external source by XX/XX/XX.	Decrease to 4 hours in the next 4 weeks (32-36 hrs. savings, $150 savings in mailing costs, and $400 in material costs. $150 increase in external labor costs).
Objectives. Dimension. Frequency. Staffing. Training. Trial period. Authority.	Alignment with team objectives and priorities.	**Reshape and Reassign** to Administrator. (Accelerate plans and schedules. Make Administrator the lead. Get external help to program system changes.)	Revise project plan, schedule and roles by XX/XX/XX. Secure contract with external source by XX/XX/XX. Notify customers on enrollment procedures through contracts, marketing literature, etc., by XX/XX/XX.	Increase to 6-8 hours per week in the next 3 weeks (2-4 hrs. more and $520 increase in external labor costs), and then average 5 hrs. per week. Yet, potential 8-12 hrs. savings for Consultants per week after start-up.

TEAM TRANSITION

Team: TSS

Member: Roger Jeffries

	PRESENT PERFORMANCE RECORD		PROGRESS REPORT
Key Functions	Key Responsibilities	Key Measurements & Methods	(Optional)
Program sales.	Seek and close direct sales of programs.	Sales volume, revenues and profits documented in weekly sales reports, meet sales goals. Recontracts. Customer feedback.	N/A
Program scheduling and enrollment.	Coordinate schedules and resource allocations.	Compliance and fulfilment of contractual obligations. Adequate and appropriate resources allocated per Director's review.	Need to schedule six new contracts.

WORSHEET

Role/Position: Training Consultant   Date: 10-1-XX

FUTURE TRANSITION PLAN

Potentially Negotiable Components	Core Needs & Filters	Negotiated Changes (Eliminate, Reshape, Reassign)	Required Actions	Targeted Results (Savings, Impacts, Etc.)
Focus. Authority. Reporting. Format. Frequency. Availability. Compliance. Customer satisfaction.	Alignment with team objectives and priorities, and new staffing constraints.	**Reshape.** (Expand sales focus to include products. Give full authority to Consultants to approve and close all sales contracts themselves. Revise the sales report to a simple format.)	Cross-train with Developers on products and programs to sell by XX/XX/XX. Revise sales report by XX/XX/XX.	Decrease to 6 hours per week (2 hrs. savings). Meet current sales forecasts through XX/XX/XX.
Contract clauses and amendments. Compliance. Customer satisfaction. Staffing. Timeliness.	Alignment with company goals, team objectives, and priorities, and new staffing and budget constraints.	**Reassign "as is"** to Director.	Forward all files to the Director by XX/XX/XX. Conduct team meeting on XX/XX/XX to discuss scheduling needs for the next 1.5 yrs. as operations are phased out.	Decrease to 0 hours per week (2 hr. savings).

Quite a bit was accomplished . . .

in the first few meetings. Key responsibilities were eliminated, rehaped and/or reassigned *"as is"* to each remaining employee. Tasks and projects were renegotiated and shifted between the Director, Consultants, Developers and the Administrator. Everyone worked hard as a team during the transition, and yet took time to celebrate with the exiting employees in their last week.

David scheduled brief 30-minute meetings every Friday for a month for the team to discuss new needs, concerns, questions or details that may have been overlooked. He also monitored the group closely to ensure no one was over- or under-utilized. After more tweaking of plans and renegotiating of agreements, he asked everyone to create a new Present Performance Record—and re-created the team.

TEAM TRANSITION WORKSHEET								
Team: _____ Member: _____ Role/Position: _____						Page: _____ Date: _____		
PRESENT PERFORMANCE RECORD			PROGRESS REPORT	FUTURE TRANSITION PLAN				
Key Functions	Key Responsibilities	Key Measurements & Methods	Optional	Potentially Negotiable Components	Core Needs & Plans	Negotiated Changes (Eliminate, Reshape, Reassign)	Required Actions	Targeted Results (Savings, Impacts, Etc.)

The Team Transition Worksheet functions as the map for bridging the team transition. Team members are now in a position to start navigating the transition as presented in the next chapter.

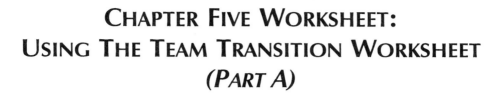

CHAPTER FIVE WORKSHEET:
USING THE TEAM TRANSITION WORKSHEET
(PART A)

Identify one employee who is leaving your work team. If there are none, focus on your job for this exercise. Using the Team Transition Worksheet provided on the following pages, complete the following sections:

Present Performance Record

1. List at least two key functions for this position.

2. For each of these functions, list at least one key responsibility, task, or project that has a high potential for being eliminated or reshaped/reassigned after further analysis.

3. List at least two measurements and methods for each of these responsibilities.

Progress Report *(Optional)*

4. For each responsibility that is a special project or task, briefly complete a progress report on its status.

Note: You will be completing page 79, the *"Future Transaction Plan,"* after Chapter Six.

TEAM TRANSITION

Team: _____

Member: _____

PRESENT PERFORMANCE RECORD			PROGRESS REPORT
Key Functions	Key Responsibilities	Key Measurements & Methods	(Optional)

WORKSHEET

Role/Position: _____

Page: _____

Date: _____

FUTURE TRANSITION PLAN

Potentially Negotiable Components	Core Needs & Filters	Negotiated Changes (Eliminate, Reshape, Reassign)	Required Actions	Targeted Results (Savings, Impacts, Etc.)

PHASE THREE: NAVIGATING THE TRANSITION

 "The real voyage of discovery consists not in seeking new landscapes but in having new eyes."

Marcel Proust

Preparing

Evaluating — Mapping

NAVIGATING

Navigating the team transition will take you from where you are to where you want to be. You will be using your map. You will be crossing the bridge.

How To Enhance Your Future Transition Plans

As you navigate your team's transition, keep a few pointers in mind.

How To Enhance Future Transition Plans

↪ **See negotiable components in everything you do**

↪ **Strengthen the connection between negotiable components and core needs**

↪ **Tap all resources to assist your team transition *(before it's too late)***

↪ **Identify core needs to reach mutual satisfaction**

↪ **Recheck core needs continually**

↪ **Don't make *"big picture"* decisions with a few puzzle pieces**

↪ **Be creative to avoid quick judgments**

↪ **Develop new *"zero-based"* performance plans**

See negotiable components in everything you do

Negotiable components are elements of a task that your team can rearrange after discussion to satisfy all parties. They are the cornerstones of any successful team transition. To further illustrate this concept, consider the following simple example.

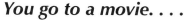

You go to a movie. . . .

In part, you associate enjoyment of the movie with eating popcorn. You have recently learned that movie popcorn is high in fat and calories and want to cut back where you can.

You could make the choices others make:

1. Eliminate it. *(Seems noble at first, but it doesn't address one core need— something to eat—and will be hard to stick to.)*

2. Make your regular order *"as is."* *(Although this meets one core need, you may later regret passing an easy opportunity to cut back on the fat, calories . . . and guilt!)*

3. Order the *"Monster Size"* and skip breakfast. *(If this is your choice, you're reading the wrong guidebook!)*

You decide to identify potentially negotiable components to satisfy your need for something to eat while watching the movie. You think of several ways to negotiate components *(with your conscience)* and minimize fat and calories:

➜ Order a smaller size container.

➜ Eliminate or reduce the amount of extra butter poured on.

➜ Share it with someone.

➜ Eat some now and take the rest home to replace a second snack.

➜ Bring your own air-popped popcorn.

➜ Substitute with frozen yogurt, vegetables, sugarless gum, etc.

As you see, there are many negotiable components that you could consider to reshape the *"task"* *(eating popcorn)* and meet the *"customer's core needs"* *(your mind and belly want something to eat while watching a movie)*. You choose to eliminate the extra butter and to order a smaller size. You saved 8.2 million calories in less than one minute!

This process is similar to negotiating components of a task at work. If it's not used, you will go blindly through work saying *"yes"* or *"no"* to new tasks coming your way *"as is"* without looking for the optimal package you may be happier *"purchasing."*

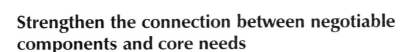
Strengthen the connection between negotiable components and core needs

Focusing on negotiable components is important, but be careful not to lose sight of the underlying needs.

Assume you were feeling burned-out . . .

on the job, and wanted to arrange for a quick, get-away-from-it-all trip. Initially, you see these negotiable components:

➜ How far should I go?

➜ How long should I stay?

➜ What method of travel should I use?

➜ When should I go?

➜ Who will go with me?

➜ Where should I stay?

➜ What activities should I plan?

But, what are your core needs? Your core needs are rest and relaxation. And you don't really care how—a trip was only an initial thought!

Recognizing this fact will stimulate you to think of more negotiable components for consideration, and more ways to satisfy your core needs, such as taking walks during breaks, getting help with complex tasks, or renegotiating project expectations (e.g. deliverables, deadlines, etc.).

You can use this process of identifying the core needs and negotiable components as you complete a transition plan for yourself—mapping a course for more rest and relaxation.

Tap all resources to assist your team transition
(before it's too late)

CarRing, an auto parts chain, . . .

was reducing staff through attrition. John had been a quiet and conscientious employee for almost a decade. He was planning to retire in one month. During the past eight years he had generated inventory reports and distributed them as requested. He often wondered why they were generated weekly and why eight pages of data was required. He also wondered why the supervisor directed him to deliver the reports to 20 people, most of whom never read them. Three managers shared with John that they only really used what was on Page 3—the rest they *"couldn't read or trust."*

At one point John almost suggested a monthly limited distribution of a single one-page summary of inventory turns. He also wanted to suggest an alternative—that the information be available on-line or to anyone upon request. No one asked for his suggestions, so he decided not to say anything. His colleagues gave him a plaque in appreciation of his years of good work, and he was on his way. Kelly, a peer, got stuck with the job of generating and distributing inventory reports *"as is."*

No one tapped John as a resource. He would have been able to help streamline his tasks by explaining what could be eliminated or reshaped while still meeting the core customer *(store managers)* needs for accurate and easy-to-reference data. CarRing's core customers were sad to see John go and were a bit distant with Kelly. She decided to lay low and *"do what's always been done."* . . .

Identify core needs to reach mutual satisfaction

Ask: *"What core needs are we satisfying with each and every task for which we are responsible?"* *"Can we satisfy these needs more efficiently?"*

Consider the needs . . .

for that inventory report John distributed weekly to 20 people at CarRing. John understood that the core need was the quick availability of accurate inventory information to maintain inventory at acceptable levels, and to locate inventory at various stores. Since parts and supplies for inventory were purchased regularly, John recognized that any report could be considered *"old"* once the print button is pressed. Therefore, getting the information on-line would meet most everyone's needs. And a one-page executive summary of monthly inventory turns could be distributed to the few senior managers who didn't use a computer.

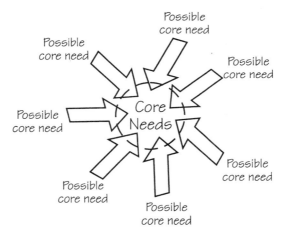

Determining needs may involve some research. Speak with those involved in the task. Look for clues, trends, motivators. Look for nonverbal cues. Paraphrase disclosures. Reflect the implications and underlying feelings. Probe further. Give people an opportunity to talk, while you actively listen. Allow them to volunteer information.

Ask, *"Is there any more you can tell me about this responsibility or task?"* Ask for their recommendations. Test your assumptions with targeted questions. Summarize what you heard.

A list of potential core needs follows. Remember that some of the most powerful motivators are the basic human needs on this list.

Potential Core Needs

- ☑ Ability to participate and share
- ☑ Affordable product or service
- ☑ Breadth of customer support
- ☑ Current, accurate information
- ☑ Empathy
- ☑ Enjoyment
- ☑ Equal opportunity
- ☑ Knowledge/training
- ☑ Power
- ☑ Professional growth
- ☑ Recognition and respect
- ☑ Quality
- ☑ Satisfaction of ethical concerns
- ☑ Satisfaction of legal requirements
- ☑ Security or stability
- ☑ Sense of comfort/confidence
- ☑ Timely, reliable services

Recheck core needs continually

Continually examine the core need or interest behind a method or task. It can keep you from making false assumptions and regrettable decisions during team transitions.

You observe a young woman . . .

catching fish. She consistently throws back any fish she catches over 11 inches in length while keeping the shorter ones.

You approach her in bewilderment. When you ask why she did this, she tells you that her grandmother, who taught her to fish, always did this.

"OK," you respond, *"but why did your grandmother throw back the longer ones?"*

"Because Nana's biggest frying pan was only 11 inches wide."

We need to pause once in a while and recheck what we were previously sure we knew.

Don't make *"big picture"* decisions with a few puzzle pieces

When completing the Future Transition Plan section of the Worksheet, it's crucial to review all current responsibilities of *all* team members. Don't make the mistake of just looking at the Present Performance Record for *"the new guy or the guy that's bailing."*

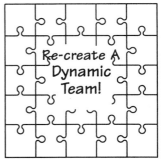

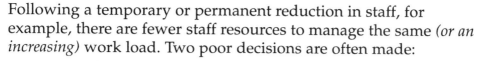
Following a temporary or permanent reduction in staff, for example, there are fewer staff resources to manage the same *(or an increasing)* work load. Two poor decisions are often made:

 The exiting employee's responsibilities are divided *"as is"* among the remaining employees, and/or,

 Only the exiting employee's responsibilities are considered for elimination.

Worse yet, these decisions are often based on erroneous assumptions:

 Each remaining employee has the free time to do more.

 All of the tasks currently managed by each remaining employee must continue to be done *"as is"*.

 All of the exiting employee's tasks that are reassigned *"as is"* cannot in any way be done differently.

 All of the exiting employee's tasks that are eliminated are of lesser importance than any other responsibility of any remaining employee.

It's a lot to swallow. Yet, as ludicrous as it sounds, these costly decisions based on gross assumptions are made every day. Why? To save time?

Be creative to avoid quick judgments

Resist the feeling that there's no time to consider other options. Ensure others don't jump to quick action plans without some discussion.

This may happen for many reasons:

 Everyone feels so overburdened that they don't feel they have the time for these discussions.

 The team leader may lack confidence and doesn't want to share the responsibility for resource allocation.

 Team members remain passive and don't speak up for fear of losing their own jobs.

 There's an air of arrogance that everyone is doing such important work—it's inconceivable to think that anyone might be doing something that could be streamlined or eliminated.

 People are getting impatient.

All pretty understandable on the surface. All pretty sad in the end. And all pay the price.

When considering negotiable components, suspend judgment. Remember that this is a list of *potentially* negotiable components—the team can later agree on what can and should be done with each key responsibility.

Completing the Future Transition Plan requires the most creativity of the whole transition process. Stretch your thinking. Look *"outside the box"* of ways things have always been done. Temporarily abandon assumptions about the way business must be done.

Regular Ways of Thinking

Develop new *"zero-based"* performance plans

Teams that have been reduced in size should *not* automatically assume that all of the present tasks should be completed in the same way or at all in the future. Circumstances have changed. So should the team. Learn to successfully play the cards that life deals to you.

When your team experiences a reduction in staff, consider developing a new *"zero-based"* Present Performance Record for all functions in the team's control. In essence, lay all of your team's functions, responsibilities, measurements and methods *"on the table."* Look at those from exiting members, new members and remaining members together. Forget *"who did what when how and why"* for now.

Now look around at your new staff resources and your new strategic directions. Ask yourself and/or your teammates: *"Given our new future plans and resources, what can we eliminate from the table? What can we change (or reshape) on the table before we take it back (e.g., Can we negotiate for more authority? Can we discard a few of the forms? Can we eliminate a few of the procedures? Etc.)? What must we take off the table "as is" and put back into our courts? What do we do with what's left over? Can we transfer these 'leftovers' to another team?"*

This process will allow a team to re-create itself. Everyone will know what they are to do and why. All options are discussed. No assumptions are made.

How To Implement Your Plans

Once your team has completed its discussions on the Team Transition Worksheets, you're ready to put your Future Transition Plan into play. Three critical steps follow.

1. **Develop new Present Performance Records**

2. **Set milestones**

3. **Communicate new roles**

Develop new Present Performance Records

Incorporate the Negotiated Changes into new Performance Records for each remaining employee. Post these so all team members can see the relationships of their responsibilities to others, and can offer suggestions for further revisions as necessary.

Set milestones

Not only are few plans perfect, but the world continues to change. Be smart. Proactively schedule regular team meetings *(e.g., every*

two weeks) to review the progress of your Required Actions, the accuracy of your Targeted Results, and the effectiveness of your new Present Performance Records.

Continue to reshape responsibilities by reconsidering negotiable components as often as is possible and necessary.

Communicate new roles

Communicate your team's new roles and responsibilities to management, other teams, and your internal and external customers and suppliers. Let them know you are open for feedback and are flexible in that you seek to continuously improve the way your team operates. Nothing should be presented in concrete.

In this chapter, you learned more about the process of determining customers' core needs and using potentially negotiable components to eliminate, reshape, or reassign responsibilities *"as is."* You also learned how to implement your plans to re-create your team. Your team is now in a position to go to the final stage of navigating the transition: Evaluating the Future Transition Plan.

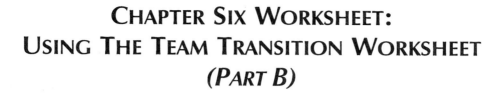
CHAPTER SIX WORKSHEET:
USING THE TEAM TRANSITION WORKSHEET
(PART B)

Continue using the Team Transition Worksheet provided at the end of Chapter Five, and complete the following sections.

Future Transition Plan

1. Pick one key responsibility and its related Present Performance Record and Progress Report.

2. Brainstorm the potentially negotiable components of this responsibility. List these directly on the worksheet.

3. Determine and add the core need(s) to your worksheet.

4. Assess the responsibility and make an initial decision for a change to be negotiated *(e.g., eliminate, reshape, or reassign "as is")*. Note this on your worksheet. *(For "reshaped" tasks, remember to also list the negotiable components of the task that are to be reshaped before the responsibility is reassigned.)*

5. Identify and document the required actions to successfully orchestrate this transition of the task.

6. Set targeted results to help you assess your progress and success.

PHASE FOUR:
EVALUATING THE TRANSITION

Preparing

EVALUATING

Mapping

Navigating

Your team starts to implement the Future Transition Plans. You've eliminated, reshaped, or reassigned responsibilities. Parts of the implementation appear to be going smoothly. Other parts need some fine-tuning.

Don't worry. You're on track. It's normal to experience a few challenges. Expect the unexpected. What's critical, however, is to track the implementation of the plan. Look for unanticipated results or consequences. You will then be in a position to make adjustments as necessary.

What To Learn From Other Travelers

Learn some valuable lessons from other travelers. Be aware of and avoid some common obstacles by constantly evaluating and re-navigating your trip.

Common Obstacles During Transitions

ᐳ **Waiting outside an open door**

ᐳ **Watching a priceless plan turn worthless without action**

ᐳ **Topping off the tank**

ᐳ **Forgetting to barter with a martyr**

ᐳ **Dumping plans on affected parties**

ᐳ **Overlooking a detail—the customer**

ᐳ **Missing the target with results**

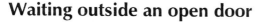
Waiting outside an open door

If you hesitate before starting to plan for a team transition, prepare to miss some opportunities. Or, prepare to be missed altogether. The door could close in front of you as you wait.

Kyle heads up Finance . . .

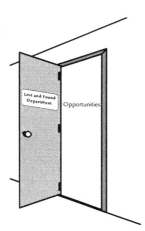

at BrainTrust, a retail management consulting firm. BrainTrust was acquired by another consulting firm, Retailers Resources Inc. Kyle was concerned since they had a Finance department of their own. Yet he knew he and his staff had more experience with the financial software packages used by both firms. He decided to wait to see what happened after the dust settled before starting the Team Transition Worksheet.

Retailers Resources' management team moved quickly. They kept those employees they knew and began streamlining the staff through layoffs. By waiting, Kyle lost an opportunity to illustrate *(and sell)* the value he and his department could have had to the new organization.

At a minimum, he could have enlightened the new management team about his team's impressive Present Performance Record. He could have presented and negotiated staffing options that took advantage of his and his team's strengths. He could have written plans and proposals. Now he finds himself writing resumes.

Watching a priceless plan turn worthless without action

Planning efforts are wasted unless the same energy is focused on the implementation and evaluation of the plan. You're on the road. You've got a map. Now just take it out of the glove compartment and use it.

Crudgo Enterprises, a fast growing. . .

waste control firm, has just received a large contract. The environmental engineers completed a Team Transition Worksheet to ensure smooth operations.

They discovered that the amount of time available to answer calls from one another is one negotiable component worthy of further scrutiny. If they had fewer interruptions, they reasoned, they would accomplish more—especially the additional goals of the new contract.

Voice mail was installed to eliminate interruptions and to take messages. Calls could now be returned at a more convenient time—for the engineers.

Some of the engineers rolled their phones over to voice mail for days on end before checking messages. Many of the new client's requests for urgent assistance went unanswered. Relationships suffered and the contract was put in jeopardy.

The engineers had not fully considered the core needs nor the impacts of their actions on internal and external customers. They did not develop measurements and expectations for returning messages. For instance, if an expectation was to return all messages within the same business day, the response from customers may have been different. Also, they could've altered the action plan so that the outgoing voice mail message included a number to call for urgent communication.

Implementing required actions and checking progress against targeted results are essential for success. The transition plan cannot otherwise jump off the paper and positively impact your work environment.

Topping off the tank

Reassigning responsibilities *"as is"* should be the last resort, *not* the first.

Whenever there are shifts in team membership, avoid the predictable pattern of reassigning exiting team members' responsibilities *"as is"* to remaining team members without discussion. It is likely that their tanks are full—and topping off a tank can be a dangerous practice.

A member of the Human Resources team . . .

at the Paradise, a gambling casino and hotel, accepted a position with another outfit. Kaye, the Human Resources manager, assembled her staff  and announced that this departing member would not be replaced. Instead, she handed out a list of his past responsibilities. In the far column of the chart was noted an employee's name who was to receive each additional responsibility *"as is."* No discussion. Not even eye contact.

Since it was the tourist season, everyone was already on edge from working long hours under tremendous pressure. This handout was the lit fuse. The bomb went off. Employees went ballistic in the meeting—one even stormed out of the room. Kaye was at a loss for words. The team was simply at a loss.

Be sure to use negotiable components to help you and your team reshape tasks and prevent an already overburdened team from taking on more work than can be handled.

Forgetting to barter with a martyr

Be cautious of overzealous team members who take on too many reassigned responsibilities.

If a remaining team member assumes too many reassigned tasks, something may be compromised. Service may decline, quality may suffer, or the team member may burn-out.

Terri is an energetic employee . . .

of the City Parks and Recreation Department. She wants to be the next in line for a promotion. The City has a hiring freeze.

Whenever the team leader assigns new responsibilities, Terri is the first to volunteer. While focusing on her new responsibilities, Terri has fallen behind on her regular tasks.

For example, her recent efforts on a research project on new playground equipment caused her to get quite behind on her schedule to trim trees. Terri had to push out her schedules—and she didn't look at the master calendar to see if there would be any conflicts. On the day of the picnic celebrating the opening of a new hospital, the noise from the rescheduled tree trimming disrupted the ceremonial speeches and award presentations. Several small children were also frightened by the noise. Numerous complaints were registered with the city.

If the quality of your product or service is negatively affected, you must make adjustments immediately. In addition, you must encourage team members to pace themselves and admit when they have taken on too much.

Dumping plans on affected parties

Involving outsiders can cost you time. You may want to pay this price now. Failure to involve everyone in the planning process who may be affected by the team transition can later cost you their support.

People who are not involved in the transition process are more likely to resist changes. If they are involved, or at least informed about your team transition, they are more likely to accept it. In addition, they will feel like active participants rather than *"victims"* of the change.

The management of The Screening Room, . . .

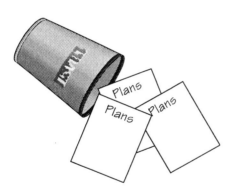

a privately owned movie theater faced with tough competition, decided it would be more profitable to divide their theater in half to show two different movies. Management announced the changes to the staff along with information on changing work shifts and the elimination of the employee lounge.

Employees were livid over the loss of the employee lounge. Instead of understanding and cooperating, some of the employees were openly resentful.

Harriet, a long-time usher, threatened to leave. *"We didn't even know they were considering the change,"* she said. *"No one asked us what we thought, or told us why they were doing it. They just said that the lounge was no longer seen as a priority. The unique charm of this historic movie house will be lost. Once again, we're treated like fat in their popcorn—ignored for someone else to cut out."*

Be sure to involve everyone affected by the upcoming change in the process, even if it means just keeping them in the communication loop *(e.g., a quick bulletin, note, memo, etc.)*. Ask for their input when possible or appropriate. Use all team members as valuable resources.

Overlooking a detail — the customer

Sometimes a team is in complete agreement on which components are negotiable. The changes in the Team Transition Worksheet may streamline their tasks and responsibilities. However, they may not have considered the impact of these changes on their customers.

Struggling to stay within budget, . . .

the Foothill Ranch Community College *(FRCC)* staff decided to close the administrative offices completely for the last week of December. When they reopened on January 2, they received numerous complaints from local citizens who had planned to register and purchase books for the spring semester. Some decided to go to neighboring colleges to pick up their electives, resulting in lost revenues for the FRCC.

The staff renegotiated the components of staffing and scheduling. In consideration of customer input, the registration office and bookstore were kept open the following year with swing shifts and skeletal work forces.

Always keep customers in mind when planning changes. You may even wish to check with customers before making a change to determine the impact on them, and then adjust accordingly.

Missing the target with results

Even in the best planned transitions, there may be unexpected consequences.

If a team does not monitor the implementation of the Future Transition Plan, a product or service may be compromised with very negative consequences. In addition, if a team does not evaluate and recognize lessons learned from the transition process, it may repeat the same mistakes in the next transition.

The Accounts Payable department . . .

of SPORDO'S, a sporting goods manufacturer, in an effort to use its time more efficiently, notified suppliers that payments would be made every six weeks instead of every two weeks. Although the manufacturer saved time, paperwork and postage, the change created cash flow problems for several suppliers and resulted in ill feelings. Two suppliers threatened to put a hold on all future shipments.

Mistakes are made. They're acceptable, but failing to learn from mistakes is not. Be open and prepared to adjust your Future Transition Plans as often as necessary, and note your changes to help you later.

How To Get Ready For The Next Team Transition

Learn from the past. Evaluate your team transitions to get ready for future evolutions. Review the success of two processes:

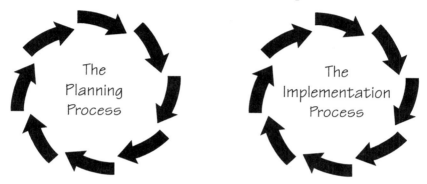

Key questions follow for your consideration.

Evaluating the planning process

☐ 1. How open were the lines of communication?

☐ 2. How effectively were expectations clarified and addressed?

☐ 3. How well did everyone initially complete the Team Transition Worksheet?

☐ 4. How much did everyone get involved in the discussion of the worksheet, and the completion of the Future Transition Plan?

☐ 5. Did everyone understand and use the concept of negotiable components?

☐ 6. Did everyone identify effective new measurements and methods to assess progress with their new performance plans?

Evaluating the implementation process

Be aware that some of the changes might require that the people involved learn new skills. Training and follow-up coaching may be necessary to reach the desired level of competence. Do not underestimate the time needed for learning and attaining the required level of competence.

☐ 1. Where did we meet and not meet the plan?

☐ 2. Are core needs being met?

☐ 3. How are customers reacting to the changes?

☐ 4. Do we need to renegotiate some of the negotiable components?

☐ 5. Did all team members remain sensitive and flexible during the transition?

There are several ways to gain valuable feedback about your team's transition process:

Feedback

1. Use direct observation to see for yourself how things are going.

2. Initiate group discussions regarding the transition process.

3. Survey team members and internal and external customers.

4. Take advantage of regular team meetings, and the hot-line, newsletter, and suggestion box.

The next team transition will come soon, so it is important to fine-tune the transition process by examining the lessons learned.

Your team members now have some proficiency using the Team Transition Worksheet. Since they now understand the concept of negotiable components, they will approach the upcoming transitions with a new frame of reference. Hopefully, all team members will proactively offer ideas and solutions that will help the entire team function more efficiently throughout future transitions.

Lastly, remember to take time to celebrate the completed transition. Share your appreciation for the hard work and creativity of all team members! Celebrate a win!

CHAPTER SEVEN WORKSHEET:
EVALUATING TRANSITIONS GONE ASTRAY
(AND NAVIGATING TOWARD SOLID GROUND)

Three of the common and significant challenges that you may encounter as you implement your Future Transition Plans are described below. Discuss and note ways your team may avoid or overcome each challenge.

1. **Challenge:** Your team is preparing for a transition following a reduction in staff. Time is running short as you ask an exiting employee *(a peer)* for his input on the Team Transition Worksheet. He says he'll get to it soon, but seems to be putting it off. As time passes, you observe this employee slowing down his pace and counting the days until he leaves. If you do not get his input, you will be left with a box of files and his telephone ringing off the hook.

   Ways to avoid or overcome:

   _____

   _____

   _____

   _____

   _____

2. **Challenge:** Your team has reshaped and reassigned responsibilities following a reorganization. Some projects had to be eliminated. Other tasks had to be postponed. As you announce your changes to other teams, you meet great resistance. Several team leaders of other departments want your team to maintain the same service levels.

Ways to avoid or overcome:

_____

_____

_____

_____

_____

3. **Challenge:** Another team agreed to take on some of your team's responsibilities to help out during a heavy growth period. Two weeks later, when *they* feel overloaded with new priorities, they eliminate some responsibilities—the ones your team reassigned to them! There was no warning. No discussion. Just a flippant, *"You want it back, you got it!"* Other departments are counting on these tasks getting done, and the ball is unexpectedly back in your court.

Ways to avoid or overcome:

_____

_____

_____

_____

_____

CHAPTER EIGHT

SUMMARY

Teams are continually changing as organizations grow, restructure, downsize, or change membership. These transitions are times of great challenges and great opportunities. Yet challenges can be overcome and opportunities can be seized with a plan and a systematic approach. And this guidebook provides just that.

The team transition is a four-phase journey. Through early preparing and mapping to navigating and evaluating, all employees become involved in creating a new future.

PREPARING

EVALUATING  MAPPING

NAVIGATING

Planning and implementing successful team transitions requires a lot of creativity and hard work. The results of maintaining a high quality team are well worth the time and energy invested with the members, customers and suppliers.

By using the guidelines, worksheets and checklists presented in this guidebook, all those affected by change will be tapped as valuable resources, and teams will be taken to higher levels of efficiency and effectiveness.

Today, everyone can be a part of re-creating a smooth transition to a successful tomorrow.

REPRODUCIBLE FORMS
AND WORKSHEETS

The pages in the Appendix are provided for you to photocopy and use appropriately.

TEAM TRANSITION WORKSHEET

Team: _____
Member: _____

Role/Position: _____

Page: _____
Date: _____

PRESENT PERFORMANCE RECORD		PROGRESS REPORT	FUTURE TRANSITION PLAN				
Key Functions	Key Responsibilities	Key Measurements & Methods	(Optional)	Potentially Negotiable Components	Core Needs & Filters	Negotiated Changes (Eliminate, Reshape, Reassign)	Required Actions	Targeted Results (Savings, Impacts, Etc.)

Core Needs And Interests

- ❏ A feeling of competency/importance
- ❏ A sense of personal accomplishment
- ❏ Ability to participate and share
- ❏ Affordable product or service
- ❏ Breadth of customer support
- ❏ Comfort/confidence
- ❏ Compliance with legal requirements
- ❏ Current and accurate information
- ❏ Empathy
- ❏ Enjoyment
- ❏ Equal opportunity
- ❏ Flexibility; not to be locked-in (*i.e., have options*)
- ❏ Getting it over with ASAP!
- ❏ Help with a difficult decision
- ❏ Knowledge
- ❏ Long-term commitment

- ❏ No unpleasant surprises
- ❏ Personal attention
- ❏ Power
- ❏ Professional growth
- ❏ Quality
- ❏ Recognition and respect
- ❏ Relief from unnecessary work
- ❏ Risk-reduction
- ❏ Role change
- ❏ Satisfaction of ethical concerns
- ❏ Security or stability
- ❏ Stable relationship/friendship
- ❏ Timely reliable service
- ❏ To be heard and understood (*empathy*)
- ❏ Training
- ❏ Other _____
- ❏ Other _____
- ❏ Other _____

Negotiable Components
To Reshape Expectations

To reshape expectations, see if you can change any of the following negotiable components regarding your responsibility, task, project, etc. *before* you reassign it! A list of negotiable components follows. Can you think of any more?

Performance Measurements:

- ❑ 1. Accuracy (*e.g., percentage of errors, reliability of data, confidence level, etc.*)
- ❑ 2. Actual Effectiveness (*versus plan*)
- ❑ 3. Autonomy
- ❑ 4. Availability
- ❑ 5. Clarity
- ❑ 6. Compliance
- ❑ 7. Consistency
- ❑ 8. Cost
- ❑ 9. Currency (*e.g., How new is the information?*)
- ❑ 10. Customer Satisfaction
- ❑ 11. Dimension (*e.g., verbal, written, on-line, etc.*)
- ❑ 12. Ease Of Reference
- ❑ 13. Employee Satisfaction
- ❑ 14. Follow-through
- ❑ 15. Frequency
- ❑ 16. Functionality
- ❑ 17. Format
- ❑ 18. Price
- ❑ 19. Quantity
- ❑ 20. Responsiveness
- ❑ 21. Scope
- ❑ 22. Timeliness (*e.g., lead time, response time, down time, cycle time, etc.*)
- ❑ 23. Thoroughness (*or completeness*)
- ❑ 24. Yield (*e.g., profit, ROI, volume, etc.*)

Other Negotiables:

- ❑ Accessories
- ❑ Authority
- ❑ Background Data/ Records
- ❑ Business Referrals
- ❑ Cancellation Clause
- ❑ Contract Clauses/ Amendments
- ❑ Costs
- ❑ Delivery (*schedule, method, costs, etc.*)
- ❑ Documentation
- ❑ Equipment
- ❑ Executive Review
- ❑ Expenses
- ❑ Fees
- ❑ Financial Review
- ❑ Focus
- ❑ Goodwill
- ❑ Guarantees
- ❑ Incentives
- ❑ Inspection
- ❑ Installation
- ❑ Jurisdiction
- ❑ Labor Costs
- ❑ Labor Schedules
- ❑ Labor/Assistance
- ❑ Legal Review
- ❑ Length of Agreement/ Contract
- ❑ Money/Price
- ❑ Necessity

- ❑ Objectives
- ❑ Options
- ❑ Packaging
- ❑ Payment Schedule
- ❑ Payment Terms
- ❑ Penalties
- ❑ Performance Standards
- ❑ Personal Attention
- ❑ Policies
- ❑ Procedures
- ❑ Profit Margin
- ❑ Quality
- ❑ Quantity
- ❑ Replacement Parts/ Spares
- ❑ Reporting
- ❑ Resources
- ❑ Return Policy
- ❑ Risk
- ❑ Service/Maintenance
- ❑ Shipping
- ❑ Specifications
- ❑ Staffing
- ❑ Time of Agreement/ Purchase
- ❑ Trade-ins
- ❑ Training/Knowledge
- ❑ Trial Periods
- ❑ Upgrades
- ❑ Warranty
- ❑ _____
- ❑ _____

THE PRACTICAL GUIDEBOOK COLLECTION FROM RICHARD CHANG ASSOCIATES, INC. PUBLICATIONS DIVISION

Our Practical Guidebook Collection is growing to meet the challenges of the ever-changing workplace of the 90's. Look for these and other titles from Richard Chang Associates, Inc. on your bookstore shelves and in book catalogs.

QUALITY IMPROVEMENT SERIES

- Meetings That Work!
- Continuous Improvement Tools Volume 1
- Continuous Improvement Tools Volume 2
- Step-By-Step Problem Solving
- Satisfying Internal Customers First!
- Continuous Process Improvement
- Improving Through Benchmarking
- Succeeding As A Self-Managed Team
- Reengineering In Action

MANAGEMENT SKILLS SERIES

- Coaching Through Effective Feedback
- Expanding Leadership Impact
- Mastering Change Management
- On-The-Job Orientation And Training
- Recreating Teams During Transitions

HIGH PERFORMANCE TEAM SERIES

- Success Through Teamwork
- Team Decision-Making Techniques
- Measuring Team Performance
- Building A Dynamic Team

HIGH-IMPACT TRAINING SERIES

- Creating High-Impact Training
- Identifying Targeted Training Needs
- Applying Successful Training Techniques
- Measuring The Impact Of Training
- Make Your Training Results Last

ADDITIONAL RESOURCES
FROM RICHARD CHANG ASSOCIATES, INC.

Improve your training sessions and seminars with the ideal tools—videos from Richard Chang Associates, Inc. You and your team will easily relate to the portrayals of real-life workplace situations. You can apply our innovative techniques to your own situations for immediate results.

TRAINING VIDEOTAPES

Mastering Change Management*
Turning Obstacles Into Opportunities

Step-By-Step Problem Solving*
A Practical Approach To Solving Problems On The Job

Quality: You Don't Have To Be Sick To Get Better**
Individuals Do Make a Difference

Achieving Results Through Quality Improvement**

*Authored by Dr. Richard Chang and produced by Double Vision Studios.
**Produced by American Media Inc. in conjunction with Richard Chang Associates, Inc.
  Each video includes a Facilitator's Guide.

"THE HUMAN EDGE SERIES" VIDEOTAPES

Total Quality: Myths, Methods, Or Miracles
Featuring Drs. Ken Blanchard and Richard Chang

Empowering The Quality Effort
Featuring Drs. Ken Blanchard and Richard Chang

Produced by Double Vision Studios.

"THE TOTAL QUALITY SERIES"
TRAINING VIDEOTAPES AND WORKBOOKS

Building Commitment *(Telly Award Winner)*
How To Build Greater Commitment To Your TQ Efforts

Teaming Up
How To Successfully Participate On Quality-Improvement Teams

Applied Problem Solving
How To Solve Problems As An Individual Or On A Team

Self-Directed Evaluation
How To Establish Feedback Methods To Self-Monitor Improvements

Authored by Dr. Richard Chang and produced by Double Vision Studios, each videotape from *"The Total Quality Series"* includes a *Facilitator's Guide* and five *Participant Workbooks* with each purchase. Additional *Participant Workbooks* are available for purchase.

EVALUATION AND FEEDBACK FORM

We need your help to continuously improve the quality of the resources provided through the Richard Chang Associates, Inc., Publications Division. We would greatly appreciate your input and suggestions regarding this particular guidebook, as well as future guidebook interests.

Please photocopy this form before completing it, since other readers may use this guidebook. Thank you in advance for your feedback.

Guidebook Title: _____

1. Overall, how would you rate your *level of satisfaction* with this guidebook? Please circle your response.

   Extremely Dissatisfied   Satisfied   Extremely Satisfied

          1   2   3   4   5

2. What specific *concepts or methods* did you find <u>most</u> helpful?

   _____
   _____

3. What specific *concepts or methods* did you find <u>least</u> helpful?

   _____
   _____

4. As an individual who may purchase additional guidebooks in the future, what *characteristics/features/benefits* are most important to you in making a decision to purchase a guidebook *(or another similar book)*?

   _____
   _____

5. What additional *subject matter/topic areas* would you like to see addressed in future guidebooks?

   _____
   _____

Name *(optional):* _____

Address: _____

C/S/Z: _____ **Phone (   )** _____

PLEASE FAX YOUR RESPONSES TO: (714) 756-0853
OR CALL US AT: 1-800-756-8096